Praise for *Inner Vc*

D1650409

*"The whole world knows Russ Whitney
as a hard-hitting real-estate guru, but now they'll
discover the much wiser and deeper, and more Zen-like,
Russ whose advice will bring joy, hope, and inner happiness
far beyond mere financial enrichment. Russ was my mentor, and
his real estate training helped me reach financial independence. His
Inner Voice message is far more meaningful and purposeful. Besides helping
me and profoundly impacting my life, he has also helped many of my Winners'
Circle Mastermind members change their lives in a very short period of time."*
— **W. Roger Salam**, founder, Winners' Circle Mastermind Forum

*"Russ Whitney is someone who has won big and lost
big, and has found a system that works to unlock your purpose and
passion in order to bring you peace and true happiness. I have
had the good fortune of learning from Russ one on one, and now
you can benefit from his wisdom and experience in this amazing book."*
— **Larry Benet**, chief connector, Speakers and
Authors Networking Group; author of *Connection Currency:
The Fastest Way to Get What You Want in Business and in Life*

*"In your hand, you hold a book written by a
man who knows the roller coaster of life. During a
downturn, Russ recognized the power of the subconscious
mind and the always-present connection to God, which
he calls the **Inner Voice**. As Jesus states, 'The Father and I
are one.' As you read this book, you will recognize that the
spark of the Higher Power is always with you, and listening
to this power will enable you to create the life of your dreams."*
— **Klaus-Uwe Kattkus, Ph.D.**, theology professor

*"I've always been a very driven person, and
sometimes you can drive too fast. When I started
working with Russ and experiencing the **Inner Voice**,
things changed amazingly! I now feel as if I have a road map
to get where I want to be in a controlled, focused fashion. Faster
isn't always better. **Inner Voice** has been a life changer for me."*
— **Kevin Harrington**, investor "Shark" on
Shark Tank (two seasons); chairman, As Seen On TV, Inc.

INNER VOICE

ALSO BY RUSS WHITNEY

Building Wealth:
From Rags to Riches Through Real Estate

Overcoming the Hurdles and Pitfalls of Real Estate Investing

Millionaire Real Estate Mentor:
The Secrets to Financial Freedom Through Real Estate Investing

Millionaire Real Estate Mindset:
Mastering the Mental Skills to Build Your Fortune in Real Estate

The One-in-a-Million 90-Day Challenge

All of the above are available at your local bookstore,
or may be ordered by visiting **www.innervoice.com**

INNER VOICE

Unlock Your Purpose and Passion

RUSS WHITNEY

HAY HOUSE, INC.
Carlsbad, California • New York City
London • Sydney • Johannesburg
Vancouver • Hong Kong • New Delhi

First published and distributed in the United Kingdom by:
Hay House UK Ltd, Astley House, 33 Notting Hill Gate, London W11 3JQ
Tel: +44 (0)20 3675 2450; Fax: +44 (0)20 3675 2451
www.hayhouse.co.uk

Published and distributed in the United States of America by:
Hay House Inc., PO Box 5100, Carlsbad, CA 92018-5100
Tel: (1) 760 431 7695 or (800) 654 5126
Fax: (1) 760 431 6948 or (800) 650 5115
www.hayhouse.com

Published and distributed in Australia by:
Hay House Australia Ltd, 18/36 Ralph St, Alexandria NSW 2015
Tel: (61) 2 9669 4299; Fax: (61) 2 9669 4144
www.hayhouse.com.au

Published and distributed in the Republic of South Africa by:
Hay House SA (Pty) Ltd, PO Box 990, Witkoppen 2068
Tel/Fax: (27) 11 467 8904
www.hayhouse.co.za

Published and distributed in India by:
Hay House Publishers India, Muskaan Complex, Plot No.3, B-2,
Vasant Kunj, New Delhi 110 070
Tel: (91) 11 4176 1620; Fax: (91) 11 4176 1630
www.hayhouse.co.in

Distributed in Canada by:
Raincoast, 9050 Shaughnessy St, Vancouver BC V6P 6E5
Tel: (1) 604 323 7100; Fax: (1) 604 323 2600

Copyright © 2013 by Russ Whitney

The moral rights of the author have been asserted.

Cover design: Gaelyn Larrick • *Interior design:* Pamela Homan

The information given in this book should not be treated as a substitute for professional medical advice; always consult a medical practitioner. Any use of information in this book is at the reader's discretion and risk. Neither the author nor the publisher can be held responsible for any loss, claim or damage arising out of the use, or misuse, of the suggestions made, the failure to take medical advice or for any material on third party websites.

A catalogue record for this book is available from the British Library.

ISBN: 978-1-78180-235-9

Printed and bound in Great Britain by TJ International Ltd, Padstow, Cornwall.

Writing a dedication for a book is often more difficult than writing the book itself. I wanted this to be right, to be meaningful, and I had been thinking about it and laboring over it for months. The night before the deadline, I was talking with my writing partner, Jacquelyn Lynn, and she closed our conversation with this: "Russ, get yourself into a quiet place with no distractions tonight or first thing in the morning, and use the *Inner Voice* strategies. Let the answers flow, just as you suggest in the book."

It pays to follow your own advice! I did exactly as she suggested, and, within minutes, I knew what to say. I am privileged to dedicate this book to:

Carl Linder: Your phone call may have saved my life.
What you said to me was the beginning of the
journey that led to **Inner Voice**.

Richie McCanna: Your kind heart, your care for others,
and the way you can forgive and let go of resentments
are a constant reminder that for some, **Inner Voice**
is the gift given to an old soul and that for the rest of us,
it's a search for the truth.

Herman Medeiros: You are proof that sometimes
God does, indeed, send angels in human form.

José Oquendo: What can I say? And that, my lifelong friend,
says it all. You are an extraordinary spiritual counselor,
and you have taught me so much.

CONTENTS

FOREWORD BY
KEVIN HARRINGTON

During more than three decades in the international infomercial business, I've had the good fortune to work with some very successful people, including Tony Little, George Foreman, Jack LaLanne, Kris and Bruce Jenner, rapper 50 Cent, and others. In my time as an investor "shark" on the ABC television series *Shark Tank,* I had the opportunity to meet many talented businesspeople who were destined to create their own fame and fortune. But now I want to talk about an amazing person I've known for more than 25 years: Russ Whitney.

I first met Russ back in the mid-1980s, when we were both young entrepreneurs in our 20s. I'll never forget our first meeting and how I was almost overwhelmed by Russ's fiery personality. He began the meeting by showing me pictures of himself at his previous job: at a slaughterhouse! Russ didn't graduate from high school and had no formal education and little business experience. He didn't fit the mold of the people I'd been working with, and I wasn't sure he and I were going to be a good business match. But as he told me about his system for investing in real estate with little or no money, he showed a passion and drive like I'd never seen. Having become a self-made millionaire at the age of 27, he was now buying up property all over Florida.

Intrigued by his system and accomplishments, I agreed to move forward with an infomercial that marketed his training program. We both had high hopes for a huge success. I wish I could say that we hit a home run and that I was the genius behind Russ Whitney's success, but that's not how it happened. This is one of those places where Russ's story gets interesting.

Our infomercial bombed.

We were both shocked. Russ's program was the real deal. Even though I was sure it would sell, I was philosophical about the fact that it didn't, and I moved on to another product. After all, I knew from experience that 99 out of 100 infomercial products end after the first failed program. But Russ didn't know that, and he wasn't about to accept that failure as final.

Russ decided to produce another infomercial. This time, he did it his way, with his own money. He didn't use any slick sales techniques or fancy production crews. He just got in front of the camera and told people they could become wealthy just as he had done. He had cameras follow him as he demonstrated his now-famous strategies for building wealth. Looking back, this was probably one of the first reality shows. Russ is genuine, he is authentic, and people relate to him and believe him. With no capital or infomercial experience, he came into the business on his own and became a superstar.

Years passed. I was busy with my own ventures, including leading National Media Corporation to $500 million in annual sales (that company's success has been chronicled in a Harvard/MIT case study) and running HSN Direct, a joint venture with Home Shopping Network; TVGoods, Inc.; and AsSeenOnTV.com. I also helped establish the Electronic Retailing Association. But Russ and I kept in touch, so when he invited me to visit his Cape Coral, Florida, office, I accepted.

I expected to see a small office with Russ and a few helpers running around in shorts and T-shirts. To my amazement, I stepped into a professional organization, with more than 500 top-notch employees. He had taken his company public, and it had grown to $250 million in annual sales; he had sold millions of books, and 60,000 people a month were registering for his training events in seven countries.

After our meeting in Cape Coral, he flew me on his private jet to his hotel in Costa Rica, where he owned a resort and conference center on more than 5,000 acres overlooking the Pacific Ocean. At that point, he was on his way to becoming one of the wealthiest and most powerful men in America. There was no stopping Russ Whitney—or so I thought.

Shortly after that trip, things began falling apart for Russ. He was pushed out of his company, and his marriage disintegrated. A lot of people were ready to write him off. I didn't hear from him for a while. When I finally did, I wasn't sure what to expect. He told me about his years of study, his travels around the world, and his mission to find his own true purpose and to figure out how others could do the same. He introduced me to the Inner Voice program, and I was blown away. I'd been experiencing some challenges of my own, and I was able to use the Inner Voice principles and strategies to gain the clarity and direction I needed. In fact, I was able to use the Inner Voice to find the solution to a problem I thought was unsolvable.

Over the years, thousands of people have come to me seeking advice or capital, and I was glad to help. When I needed advice, I turned to Russ and the Inner Voice program.

If Russ had quit after that first infomercial failed, I wouldn't have the privilege of writing this foreword now. But Russ knew even then—consciously or not—that he was destined to do something great, that he was put here on this earth to make a difference by helping others. And he knew that there were lessons he had to learn and struggles he had to overcome to find and fulfill his purpose. His mission is not yet complete, but with this book and the Inner Voice community, he is on his way. I'm honored to be a part of *Inner Voice*, and I believe it will help you find what you're looking for. I invite you to join me on the Inner Voice journey.

INTRODUCTION

The flight from Florida to Hawaii is a long one, and I was anxious and unsure—not about the flight I was getting ready to take, but about what was going to happen after I arrived. I boarded the plane, took my seat, ordered a drink, and then dropped my head into my hands and began to cry.

I was the founder and CEO of a publicly traded international financial training organization with annual revenues of $250 million. I owned millions of dollars in real estate in the United States and abroad. I lived in a beautiful home and had a collection of expensive cars. I provided jobs for thousands of employees and independent contractors. I had helped thousands of people achieve their economic dreams.

Yet my marriage had fallen apart, my relationship with my kids was strained, and I was being forced out of the company I had created and built. And now I was on a plane headed to a treatment center in Hawaii—a place described to me as a mental, physical, and spiritual rehab facility.

I was embarrassed, confused, burned out, and tired.

What in the world had just happened to my life?

More important, why should you care? What's in it for you?

The answer to the last question is simple: After decades of teaching people how to build material wealth, a series of circumstances—some within my control and some beyond my control—taught me how to build spiritual wealth. I am now compelled to share that knowledge so that you can have the benefit without the pain. And the answer to the previous two questions is: You'll see as we go along.

Although the Inner Voice program is not about making money, it will make you rich in ways you never dreamed possible. It won't force you to make changes you don't want to make or aren't ready for, although it's there for you when you're ready. And it's not a religion, although it doesn't in any way conflict with religious principles.

Fast-Forward to Today

My very public and painful crash was an end and a beginning. I had started at the age of 20, with virtually nothing, and embarked on a quest to make money. Yet more than three decades later, even though I had plenty of money, I felt as if I were in a similar place: starting with virtually nothing and embarking on a quest to find answers. I had been brought to my knees and was forced to look outside my insulated world for understanding.

What is the meaning of life? Why are we here? What's the point of it all?

Is there a predetermined plan for our lives? And if there is, can we find out what that plan is so that we're not bouncing around like balls in a pinball machine? How do we know if we're doing what we're supposed to be doing?

My search took me around the world, where I met and studied with top business and spiritual leaders. I traveled not only across the United States, but also to Abu Dhabi, Dubai, Israel, Haiti, Colombia, the Caribbean, Central America, Brazil, Italy, France, England, Scotland, and other places. Sometimes I was alone; other times, I was with a number of life coaches and spiritual advisors so that I could continue my learning process every waking moment.

It took me five years and more than 20,000 hours to figure out what you're going to learn in the few hours it will take you to read this book. What I learned is amazing in its simplicity and power. Once I understood it, I wanted to pass it along so that others could experience the peace and joy I have come to know. When I started sharing what I had learned, something happened that I hadn't expected: The information quickly took on a life of its own. My friends have shared it with their friends, who have shared it—well, you get the idea.

My personal quest has evolved into a worldwide Inner Voice community made up of like-minded individuals who are committed to living the Inner Voice way of life and practicing the Inner Voice principles and strategies that you'll learn from this book. Those principles and strategies are new ways to handle age-old life issues that humans have always had to deal with. We might like to think that we're special, that we're different, but the reality is, we're not. Humans haven't changed much, if at all, since we made our first appearance on Earth. Five thousand years ago, the Mayan Indians were dealing with the same relationship challenges, rebellious children, pain and grief, business difficulties, and financial struggles that we are dealing with today. The only difference is that today we have modern conveniences and technology, but the fundamental challenges are essentially the same.

The Inner Voice community is an in-person, phone, and Internet-based alliance of people who are seeking personal and spiritual growth, and who understand that we cannot reach our full potential alone. When we need a deeper understanding or a simple clarification of an issue, or when we need some support to help us through a personal, business, or financial situation, we turn to the Inner Voice community.

Within that community are people of various levels of development. Some of the more experienced individuals have chosen to become Inner Voice coaches. All Inner Voice coaches are specially trained and certified to provide the specific coaching and support our community members need. Throughout this book, I'll be sharing some of my experiences as a practicing Inner Voice coach. If those stories appeal to you, you may want to explore the personal and professional opportunities that becoming an Inner Voice coach offers.

The Ground Rules

My sincere hope and wish is that, through the Inner Voice, you are able to find your purpose and then build your passion while living the free, happy, joyful life you were intended to live. But while I can show you the way, I can't drag you there—even though there was a time when I would have tried. I've come to understand, as you will, that Inner Voice is a way of life that's shared by attraction, not promotion.

Let me give you some suggestions that have helped me and others who live the Inner Voice way of life:

— **No advice or opinions.** I will tell you about my own experiences, what I learned, and why my life is better now. We call that sharing experience, strength, and hope. I won't give you my opinion of what might be happening in your life, nor will I tell you what I think you should do. If, from that, you can formulate suggestions for your own life that you put into action and that work for you, wonderful. If not, that's okay, too. The information will be there when you are ready.

— **Honesty.** Everything I tell you will be the truth as it was taught to me. You will learn why the truth is so important, even down to what you might have thought were harmless little "white lies." I will share personal things about myself that I haven't shared before, things I used to hide. I'll also tell you things about others who are living the Inner Voice way of life. All of the stories in Inner Voice either are my own or have been shared by members of the Inner Voice community, and they're true. The names have been excluded or changed to protect the privacy of our contributors and their families.

— **Only principles and strategies.** You will learn the principles you can use to improve your life and the specific strategies, or action steps, you can use to implement them. No dogma, no preaching, no judgment—just proven principles and strategies that you are free to accept or reject.

The View from 30,000 Feet

When you have put all the pieces of the puzzle together, it's easy to see the entire picture. But until you do, it might be difficult to see how it all fits. So let's get an overview of what you're going to learn.

We're going to begin by discussing the phases of life and how we operate during each phase. We'll focus on the warrior and statesperson phases: the two phases the majority of us spend most of our adult lives in. As we grow and evolve from warrior (the mode we are typically in during our younger years) to statesperson (the mode that usually comes with maturity), we begin to understand the inner voice, which is our connection to the force within and beyond ourselves that goes by a variety of religious and secular names. Our contact with the inner voice typically begins with vague thoughts that evolve into purposeful communication, and eventually we master the ability to make daily, conscious contact with our inner voice so that our lives are guided by its wisdom.

Even as we learn the importance of personal and spiritual growth, we also learn that we are designed to live in the present. When we spend time in the past or worry about the future, we find ourselves in negative, unhealthy states that, at best, are exhausting and, at worst, inflict serious damage to us and our relationships. By living in "today," we also increase our understanding of humility, powerlessness, and surrender, as well as the amazing strength and serenity that come from those principles.

Although we aren't made to live in yesterday or tomorrow, we must understand yesterday and plan for tomorrow. We need to figure out why we are who we are, how everything in our past combined to bring us to today, and how to use that knowledge to reveal our life's purpose. You'll learn how to do that with a tool called the "Discovery Chart."

The phrase "passion and purpose" has been used to the point of becoming a cliché, but the inner voice takes a fresh approach by first helping you figure out why you are here—your purpose—and then guiding you as you develop a passion for doing the things that will help you fulfill your purpose.

With this foundation of knowledge, we can understand essential life principles, Inner Voice principles, and the strategies we can use to live out those principles to our benefit. We'll also learn how to make the right decisions every day, measure our progress, and stay on track.

Finally, once you've accepted the Inner Voice gift, you'll learn how to share it with others as I'm sharing it with you, either simply as a friend or professionally as an Inner Voice coach.

Are You Ready?

When I boarded that plane to Hawaii, I had no idea what would happen to me, how my life was going to change, what I would learn, or how challenging some of the lessons would be. I had plenty of questions and very few answers. When I looked to the future, I couldn't see anything.

Today my life is spiritually richer than it's ever been. Because I'm on track with the Inner Voice program, I wake up every morning excited about what I have to do and totally at peace with how and why I'm going to do it. I know why I'm here, and I'm consumed with passion about it. What I want to share with you is an awareness, a feeling, a mind-set, an understanding of things that often seem beyond our comprehension. So if you're ready, let's begin.

TIPS FOR READING
INNER VOICE

Inner Voice is a systematic approach to a new way of life. Although the book is set up to take you sequentially through the process, when you finish reading it through the first time, it's unlikely that you'll be finished with it. It's a reference that you'll want to return to again and again.

Throughout the book, you'll see "Inner Voice Whispers." These are bits of wisdom and advice I've received through my inner voice that I wanted to share with you in a special way. Use them to guide you in your understanding of this powerful program. You'll also see "Living the Inner Voice Life." These are true, first-person stories from people who have learned and applied Inner Voice principles and strategies. They are included to show you the incredible impact the inner voice can have on your life.

I recommend that you read *Inner Voice* with a pen or highlighter handy. Mark the passages that are particularly meaningful to you. Make notes in the margins or keep a journal nearby for making notes. Dog-ear or tab the pages that you want to come back to. The key is to capture all the thoughts that come to you while you're reading. When you see something that makes you think, that causes you to recall something in your past or reflect on a situation in your present, let those thoughts complete themselves. This is part of your transition to the Inner Voice way of life.

If you see a concept that seems familiar or perhaps doesn't seem to apply to you, don't shortchange yourself by skipping past it. Take the time to read it and see how it integrates with the Inner Voice way of life: a way of life that's freer, more joyful, and far more abundant than you could ever imagine.

∞

CHAPTER ONE

WHERE ARE YOU NOW?

One of the more important discoveries I've made is that our lives can be divided into four distinct phases. It's a concept first articulated by Carl Jung (the Swiss psychotherapist and psychiatrist who founded analytical psychology) and later discussed by countless spiritual writers over the years. Jung's writing explains it using complex sentences with words and phrases like "false presupposition" and "hitherto." I'm going to do it simply.

The phases are naturally sequential in a way that's related to our level of maturity and understanding of life in general, once we grow past early childhood and enter our teen years. Although it makes sense that we would move through each phase in order, much like how we progress through grades in school, completing a phase without going back, that's not how it happens. We move in and out of the phases, and sometimes we are in more than one phase at the same time. When we understand the phases, we can better understand what motivates our actions. And when we understand what motivates our actions, we can make better choices.

The four phases are:

1. **Athlete:** This is also known as the vanity phase. It's when our focus is on ourselves and we are mostly concerned with our physical bodies and how we look. Want proof? Watch teenagers walk by a mirror; they can't do it without checking their reflection. Sometimes they're admiring, sometimes they're

critical, but they look at themselves every chance they get. And no matter what happens, their primary concern is how it impacts them. You may know some older people—adults and even senior citizens—who are this way as well. The athlete phase is an immature, self-centered mind-set that some of us never grow beyond.

2. **Warrior:** As we move into our adult years and assume greater responsibilities, we enter the warrior phase of life. This is the time when we want to conquer the world. We want to win—to be the best and have the best. We act as warriors act, and we do what warriors do. We're always prepared for battle, even when it doesn't matter and isn't necessary.

3. **Statesperson:** As we gain maturity, we evolve into the statesperson phase. As warriors, we looked out for ourselves. As a statesperson, we shift from "What's in it for me?" to "How can I make a difference and serve others?" We no longer emphasize money, power, and possessions as we once did. Certainly we accept and enjoy those things, but we know there's far more to life than that. We learn that giving is the best way to receive and that the time has come for us to take action to leave this world a better place than we found it.

4. **Spirit:** This is when we come to the ultimate realization that we are spiritual beings having a human experience, not the other way around. We understand that we are more than our bodies, more than our possessions, more than our friends and families, more than our worldly achievements. We recognize our truest essence, our highest selves.

Do you recognize yourself in one or more of those descriptions? I do. I moved into the warrior phase when I was a young husband and father at the age of 20. I was determined to get and keep my life on track, to take care of my family, to prove to the world that I was a winner. I stayed in that phase pretty much exclusively for more than three decades; then I was introduced to the statesperson phase. I'd like to say I began growing into it naturally, but the truth is that I was hammered into it by what I call a life crushing. A *life crushing* is what it says: something that crushes us. Someone (a relationship) crushes us, a devastating accident occurs, or we crush ourselves. Life crushings are always personal and relative. They might be the end of a marriage, the death of someone we love, an illness, a serious business or financial blow—the list is endless. It's important to recognize that what may crush one person is barely a blip on the radar screen to someone else, and what may have crushed you years ago won't bother you at all today. And although it took a life crushing for me to begin evolving into the statesperson phase, the process happens differently for everyone, so don't think you have to experience something awful to achieve this level of personal growth.

Every day, I feel as if I move more into statesperson, but I haven't completely shed the warrior. I'm not sure most of us ever completely move beyond the warrior phase. Even when we understand it and are committed to evolving, there will still be emotions and events that will trigger our warrior behavior. And as far as the spirit phase goes, I'm not sure I'll ever make it to that phase. Those who have reached that level include the likes of Gandhi and Mother Teresa, and I don't believe they had finished learning how to be better spiritual beings either. You'll have to do your own evaluation, but at least at this point, I don't believe reaching the spirit phase is the purpose for my life. I don't think the creator meant for this to be the goal for all of us, because we all have different purposes. As in all endeavors, there has to be a chief cook, there has to be someone to clean up after the chief cook, and someone needs to be the server. Just as we can't all be the chief cook, it's my experience that we're not all meant to reach the spirit phase permanently. Even so, I believe we should regularly pause to evaluate which phase we're in and consider what we need to do to continue our personal and spiritual development, even as we move back and forth among the phases.

Fighting the Battle, Winning the War

The two phases of life that we address in the Inner Voice program are the warrior and statesperson phases. If you're taking the time to read this book, you've already moved beyond the athlete phase. And if you've already reached the spirit phase, you know far more than I do.

When we are in the warrior phase, we do a lot of complaining when things aren't going our way. When someone disagrees with us, we go to battle—and often continue fighting even if we realize we're in the wrong. As statespersons, we learn new ways to handle our old beliefs and behaviors, including our beliefs about what we're supposed to do when things aren't going the way we think we want them to go.

Inner Voice Whispers

You can make excuses, or you can make progress. You can't make both.

The line between warrior and statesperson often looks like the edge of the water between the shore (warrior) and the ocean (statesperson). It's a line, but it's ever changing and always in motion. The shore is rigid and generally inflexible. The ocean is strong but flexible: it knows how to wrap itself around obstacles and deal with them. As you mature from warrior to statesperson, you'll find yourself moving from the beach into the water, back to the beach, and then back to the water. Gradually, you'll spend more and more time in the water.

In my younger warrior years, I thought I was always in charge—and if I felt unsure, I never let it show. I was always ready to face adversity head on, whether I knew what I was doing or not. But I was operating on the training I'd received from other people—people who were themselves probably also in their warrior phase—and I didn't know any other way to function. As a result of that arrogance—or, more accurately, ignorance—I chased more failures than I care to count.

If we are to progress from warrior to statesperson, we need to learn how to operate in statesperson mode. One of the best ways to do that is to surround ourselves with people who are already there. My life is a classic example of why that can be challenging. I was born into a middle-income, blue-collar family. My father left my mother when I was a small child. He remarried, and the woman he chose as his partner to help him raise his kids turned out to be worse than the stereotypical "stepmonster." I endured years of unspeakable abuse that only ended when I ran away at the age of 14, after my father's death.

I spent the following years on my own, without much adult supervision or guidance. I did a lot of things right—but I made some mistakes. My most serious mistake landed me in prison while I was still a teenager. What I did isn't important; what matters is that, although I didn't realize it at the time, it was probably the best thing that could have happened to me. At the age of 20, I was released from the New York State Department of Corrections and sent to Albany with $200 and a state-issued suit. I'd never been to Albany, but there I was with no friends or family, on my own after having been incarcerated for almost three years. It was a chance to start over with a clean slate, and I took it.

Despite having dropped out of high school, I'd earned my GED in prison and was able to get a factory job at a slaughterhouse. My duties included cleaning up the floor and working on a production line where about 1,400 hogs a day were butchered and packaged for grocery stores. It was nasty, dirty work—and a big break for me. It was a union job that paid decent wages (a starting rate of about $5 an hour at the time) with benefits, security, and opportunities for advancement. I saw it as the vehicle that would let me keep the promise I had made to myself while in prison: to build a decent, law-abiding, middle-class life; to own a home; to get married and have a family; and to love, nurture, and care for my wife and children.

Winning Doesn't Always Require Fighting

When I was introduced to the phases of life, the concept made sense. However, as an attorney, I knew that my clients and opposing counsel expected a warrior, a legal mercenary. And when confronted with a warrior, our first instinct is to "war" back.

Learning to stop and hear the inner voice say, "Warrior or statesperson?" has allowed me to reflect and often take a more diplomatic approach to resolving a conflict. Although, at first, I was concerned that I would appear weak and my clients wouldn't be satisfied, the reality is that the approach actually produces better results that my clients appreciate.

— David,
attorney

Within a few weeks of starting that job, I met a young lady who also worked there, and three months later, we were married. Three months after that, she got pregnant with our daughter. We were happy: young, healthy, in love, and living the only version of the American dream either of us knew. But even as it seemed as if things were as close to perfect as we could ever expect, I kept hearing a nagging voice in the back of my mind telling me, "You can do something better with your life. You can do something better with your life."

The challenge was that I didn't know what to do. I didn't know what "better" was. All I had heard growing up was that if I got a job, was dependable, took care of my family, paid my bills on time, and didn't try anything too risky, life would be good. And it was all I, as a young husband and father, heard from the people in my life at the time, including my father-in-law, whom I respected and admired. My role models were limited—and if there was a statesperson in the crowd, I didn't realize it.

But the voice wouldn't be quiet. Even though I didn't know where the voice was coming from or exactly what it wanted me to do, rather than ignore it, I listened to it. When someone gave me a magazine about business opportunities, I leafed through it and noticed all those enticing advertisements in the back. I began exploring the "get-rich" opportunities. Most of them didn't appeal to me, but I finally found one that did. It was a $10 book on real estate investing, and everything it said made complete sense to me. Even better, the strategies worked. Within two years, I was making enough money from my real estate investments to quit my job at the slaughterhouse. Four years after that, I achieved millionaire status. Yet the voice was still telling me I could do better, so I shared the story of how I accomplished such remarkable success in my first book, *Overcoming the Hurdles and Pitfalls of Real Estate Investing*, and then later in my second book, *Building Wealth*. I started a number of businesses, including a financial training organization, and wrote more books. I realized that I had a passion for teaching, for helping people learn how to improve

Inner Voice Whispers

Don't live in fear.
Live in faith and gratitude.
Fill your heart with love
and thankfulness for all that
you now have so that there
is no space left for fear.

their lives. I was doing statesperson work, but I was still solidly in warrior mode.

The Story of My Rise and Fall

My warrior self continued to charge forward. I'll be sharing more about my business adventures and misadventures as we go along. For now, it's enough to say that while not all of the dozens of businesses I either started or purchased worked, I appeared to be a classic Horatio Alger success story. I was a multimillionaire leading what looked like a charmed life. One of my most visible business achievements was building a global training company that was a leader in innovative adult financial education. I was living full-time in warrior mode, never giving myself much of a break. I lived that way for more than 12 years, and today I realize that it was inevitable that I would crash and burn.

Inner Voice Whispers

Every battle has at least one loser, but not every battle has a winner. When the fighting won't stop, everybody loses.

My marriage crumbled, and I was very publicly forced out of the company I had founded and built. But even worse was that for a while, my children were ashamed of what they saw as my failure. I clearly remember something one of them said that crushed me: "Dad, you have always been able to fix everything. Why can't you fix this?" We both cried, but at the time, I was at a total loss about what to do. I didn't know how to "fix this." The fear, helplessness, and pain were the worst I'd ever felt, close to as bad as I had felt from the abuse I'd suffered as a child, worse than what I'd suffered in prison.

I had become a recluse. I was self-medicating and drinking too much alcohol. My friends were understandably worried about me, but I blew them off. Finally I got a call that I listened to.

The caller was a friend who happened to be a high-profile attorney who handled legal affairs for me and my family. He said that in all the years he'd known me, I had never missed meetings or just not shown up to functions where I'd committed to be. I didn't want to hear it. I was starting to tune him out when he said, "Russ, I had a dream last night, and you were in it. I dreamed you, some of our friends, and I were all out having a good time. We ended up back at your house, where we fell asleep. And one of us didn't wake up."

The line went silent. Finally, I said, "The person who didn't wake up—was that me?"

He quietly answered, "Yes." He paused for another moment and then continued, "Russ, considering all you've been through, I think you need some help. You've been doing things for others your whole life. You need to take care of yourself now."

There was another long moment of silence before I promised to think about it. After we got off the phone, I talked to another friend, a doctor, and told him about the call. He said he thought I might have some serious medical issues, and he recommended that I see some specialists.

It wasn't the first time I'd heard that message, but I'd rejected it every other time it was suggested. After all, I was Russ Whitney. I had it all: wealth, success, a beautiful family, material possessions. But this time was different. Did I suddenly realize that my friends were right? Was this an unconscious contact with my inner voice? I don't know. I just know that I finally accepted that I needed help, but I didn't know where to start. My friends got together and researched facilities that could help me; agreed on a unique place in Hawaii they called a "mental, physical, and spiritual rehab"; and made the necessary arrangements for me to go there.

Just two days later, I was on a plane heading to Hawaii. Before I left, I was making jokes about it. My attitude changed once I was on the plane. The flight itself was one of the most emotionally difficult experiences of my life. Little did I know that when the plane touched down on that island paradise out in the Pacific Ocean, I would embark on a five-year journey that would change my life forever. And now, I'm hoping it will also change yours.

Not Your Typical Hawaiian Vacation

I had no idea what to expect. I didn't have an address for this secret retreat; all I knew was that it was on the island of Oahu and that anyone who was accepted by the facility would be met at the airport and driven there. The pictures I'd seen showed an ocean-front, secluded mansion with beautiful suites, a gym, and other first-class amenities. The structured program included meeting and working with various specialists, therapists, and doctors.

A key part of the process was a completely healthy diet, prepared by the on-site gourmet chef; daily exercise; plenty of sessions on the life-change process; and no intoxicants whatsoever.

What? No alcohol?

I had never been an out-of-control, excessive drinker. During most of my warrior years, I'd indulged in alcohol, but never to excess and rarely during the work week. But during the year or so before I went to Hawaii, my alcohol consumption had increased, and I wasn't comfortable with the idea that I suddenly couldn't drink at all, not even a glass of wine with dinner. Nevertheless, I was willing to give this whole program a try.

Inner Voice Whispers

You can be exceptionally kind, loving, giving, and respectful without being a slave to the opinions of others. Accept that other people will disapprove of some of the things you do, and you'll free yourself to do truly magnificent things.

At that point, even though I had lost more than 80 percent of my net worth, I still had enough resources that I didn't have to worry about doing something to make money right away. I decided that since I had been working 15-hour days, often 7 days a week, for most of my adult life, I was entitled to a break. A luxurious retreat in Hawaii was as good a place as any for a vacation, for the chance to relax and think about what I was going to do next. But I was still in warrior mode, so I approached that "break" with a warrior attitude. And if I wasn't going to get any alcohol at the retreat, it made sense to drink plenty during the flight. I got off the plane in Hawaii with a pretty good alcohol buzz; it was, after all, going to be my last hurrah before making a major life change.

After being alone for the 18-hour flight, I was having second thoughts about this whole thing when I got off the plane. I certainly didn't need any more alcohol, but I was trying to delay the inevitable, so I decided to stop at the airport bar for another drink. I'm not sure how long I stayed there or how much I had to drink, but when I finally decided to go down to baggage claim to meet my hosts, there was only one piece of luggage on the carousel. It was mine. And there were two people there to meet me, both with sincere smiles on their faces.

One was Herman, a big fellow, about six foot three, who would come to play a significant role in my life and the Inner Voice program. The other was a lovely lady I would know only briefly. Neither one of them seemed at all put out with me for having made them wait. They were as genuinely gracious and kind as they could be. I remember wondering what I'd gotten myself into and thinking that they'd better not start holding hands and singing "Kumbaya."

The man grabbed my luggage, and the woman insisted on carrying my briefcase. There was an aura of peace about them that I couldn't understand or relate to at the time—although I have since come to understand it clearly, and you will, too. We climbed into a Range Rover and headed off to the mysterious retreat. I made a few jokes about stopping somewhere for a happy-hour drink. They'd probably heard those kinds of jokes before, and they laughed with me. But we didn't stop.

We finally arrived at the secluded mansion that was going to be my home for the next few months. Although the estate was as beautiful as the pictures had indicated, I was starting to realize that this wasn't going to be a purely fun vacation. As I walked into the main building, I arrogantly demanded to see the various amenities. They showed me around, and I was critical of everything; actually, I was looking for any excuse to get out of there. I was used to being in charge, to being the leader. I didn't even know what was going to happen there, so how could I feel as if I were in control of it? I just wanted to escape and get back to a place where I could control things.

I told the two men who had greeted me at the door that I had decided to leave. I'd get a hotel room for the night and head back to Florida the next day. They seemed to understand but asked me to at least look at the suite that was ready for me. I decided it wouldn't hurt to be polite and take their brief tour—but I was still looking for opportunities to let them know that Russ Whitney didn't want or need what they had to offer. In retrospect, I have to applaud them for not laughing out loud at the absurd things I said and did. For example, as I followed them up the stairs, I noticed some small stains on the carpet and decided to announce that I was above staying in a place that wasn't absolutely perfect. I stopped, pointed at the stains, and pompously said, "Whoa! Look at those stains. I'm outta here!" I headed back down the stairs, grabbed my luggage, and was out the door in less than a minute. I asked someone to call a limo to take me to Waikiki. I could get a hotel room there, maybe spend a few days on the beach, and then make arrangements to fly home.

Looking back, I can see how irrational my behavior was. I wasn't in control, I was still feeling the effects of the alcohol I'd consumed on the plane and at the airport, and I wasn't thinking straight. It was just starting to get dark, and I headed down the long driveway to the gate, where I assumed the limo would be. I heard footsteps running behind me. It was José, one of the men who had greeted me at the door. Speaking with a thick Latin accent, he asked me to reconsider staying. I assured him that the place was not up to my standards, something that I know now wasn't true; the facility was absolutely beautiful.

José persisted. He told me about others who had experienced great success after going through the program. I continued walking to the gate. Then José started telling me about some of the high-profile executives and celebrities whose lives had been changed for the better at this retreat. He mentioned the name of a famous actor who, just the previous week, had stayed in the suite they had reserved for me. At first I had no idea whom he was talking about. When I finally realized how badly José, with his strong accent, was butchering the name of a man you would probably immediately recognize, I started to laugh—laughter that bordered on hysterical. José laughed with me. Finally, promising that this would be a life-changing experience for me, he talked me into going back inside and at least staying the night. I was still skeptical, but without my own transportation, my options were limited.

Inner Voice Whispers

Leave the world
a better place.
Be sure one life
has breathed easier
because you have lived.

Once in the suite, which was as large and elegant as the presidential suite in any first-class hotel, I realized how exhausted I was. I said a prayer and crawled into bed. I was here; what would be the harm in giving it a chance? Before I could spend any more time wondering what tomorrow would bring, I fell into a deep sleep.

When the Dawn Came

I was scheduled to be at the retreat for 45 days, with an option to stay longer if I wanted to. At that point, I had no idea how much work I had to do or how long it was going to take. I was accustomed to making quick decisions, taking immediate action, and getting quick results. I figured this experience wouldn't be much different from anything else I'd done, except that it was set against the backdrop of an exquisite Hawaiian location.

I was so wrong.

In my wildest thoughts, I had no idea that what was going to happen to me would turn into a way of life that would be more fun and more fulfilling than any amount of money or material success I'd had so far.

My first three days were occupied with medical exams, psychological evaluations, and mandatory meetings. I was cooperative, although still in warrior mode and waiting to see some evidence that this experience was what I needed.

That evidence came on the third day. I was being nagged by a very clear thought that I couldn't escape. Although it would be a while longer before I completely comprehended that this was a higher power speaking to me through my inner voice, the message was relentless: I needed to learn every bit of information that was being so freely shared by the staff and others at this retreat. I needed to make dramatic changes in my life if I wanted to reach a place of joy, contentment, and freedom in spirit. And I needed to prepare to take that knowledge to my existing audience (the more than six million people around the world who had either bought one of my earlier books or attended one of my seminars) and beyond.

From that point forward, I understood my purpose, my mission, and dedicated myself to it. I don't think my teachers and counselors—the ones at the retreat and those who came later as I continued my journey—ever had a more enthusiastic and determined student.

As I began to comprehend the magic of the inner voice, one of my biggest challenges was communicating it to others. Is it your relationship with God? Is it your subconscious? Is it some form of infinite intelligence? Is it a higher power? Is it intuition? Is it a program?

And the answer, as I would come to understand it, is yes: it is all of those things and more. And in time, I learned how to articulate it as I'm doing now. So let's talk about what the inner voice is.

CHAPTER TWO

Defining the Inner Voice

We all have an inner voice. Some of us hear it very clearly; others either ignore it or confuse it with coincidence, as I frequently did in my younger, warrior days. Before we learn how the inner voice works and start to understand its true power, we may refer to it using terms such as:

- A creative idea
- Luck
- A gut feeling
- Coincidence
- The stars being aligned
- An *aha* moment
- A guardian angel

These terms aren't wrong; they just aren't enough.

Our inner voice will give us answers, provide guidance and direction, and help us achieve our goals once we begin to recognize it as the pure guidance that it is. Most of the successful people I've worked with discover their own inner voice and are willing to learn how to let it guide them. By *successful*, I don't mean just wealthy; I mean people who have come to know their true purpose in life. It's not only that they listen to the inner voice, but that they also have a relationship with it. Yes, I know that sounds a little "out there," but it's true. You can't have a relationship of any sort—marriage, friendship, business, and so on—without communication. A relationship with the inner voice can serve all of our human relationships, enriching them in an abundance of ways. And that relationship is built through communication.

One of the ways in which I communicate with the inner voice is using a technique that I call "two-way conscious contact." I use this and other methods every day to communicate with the inner voice, and I'm going to teach you how to do it, too. I still get *aha* moments—today, I call them "Inner Voice Awakenings"—but now I know where they're coming from and how to listen to them.

I first began receiving messages from my inner voice at age 20, when I was putting my life together after being released from prison. At the time, I didn't know what the voice was; I didn't recognize it as my inner voice until many years later. Back then, my life looked decent from the outside, especially considering my background. I was married with a baby on the way, I had a decent job that was reasonably secure, and I had friends. But in spite of all that, I kept hearing a voice telling me that there was more, that I could do better. I wasn't sure what that meant, but instead of ignoring the message, I tried to figure it out. What I didn't realize until decades later was that, because I was trying to figure it out, the voice helped me along.

Today I understand that I was making unconscious contact with my inner voice, and the reason I was able to do that at such a young age is because I didn't "know" it wasn't possible. I was young, I had little in the way of formal education, and I was extremely naïve. I was in a perfect place to follow my inner voice, even though I didn't know that's what I was doing.

The more childlike we are, the more likely we are to have unconscious contact with our inner voice, because we aren't blocking the messages. We're open and receptive, because no one has told us not to be. Once people start telling us that we can and can't do certain things, that we are limited by certain restrictions, that we must follow arbitrary rules, it becomes more and more difficult to discern our inner voice. It's a lot like how we teach children to stifle their creativity by making them color within the lines or by telling them that their imaginary friends don't exist, and then we praise and reward them for conforming. People they trust tell them that being creative and different isn't acceptable, so they stop being creative and different; they shut out the inner voice that may be trying to direct them to the next great medical or technological discovery, or maybe just to a pleasurable hobby.

As my inner voice was telling me that I could do better, people around me were all too happy to point out that I couldn't, that I should be satisfied with what I had. And if I had even a little more education and worldly experience at that point, I might have agreed with them. Or I might have decided that "better" simply meant a job in management instead of cleaning the meat-packing plant floor. Instead, I let my inner voice drive me. It never occurred to me to let logic and reason muffle my inner voice.

Of course, at the time, I didn't know how to completely understand what my inner voice was telling me to do. I didn't know how to ask for more information, how to test the message, or how to confirm the accuracy of my understanding—all of the things you're going to learn in this book. I was in warrior mode, and warriors typically don't realize where the messages that inspire and guide them are coming from; that's something we often don't get until we begin to evolve into the statesperson phase. But the sooner you recognize your inner voice, the easier it will be for you to reach that phase.

Inner Voice Whispers

Life gets better when we make the decision to not worry about what others say about us. If someone talks about you, it's none of your business. Your job is to keep your side of the fence clean from the perspective of you and the God of your understanding—that's it.

Achieving Postdivorce Peace

Even though I understood the concept of the phases of life and recognized my warrior self, I couldn't stop it from affecting my relationship with my former wife. I knew that regardless of the issues that caused the breakdown of our marriage, we were good parents and blessed with two outstanding sons who have given us beautiful grandchildren. But I wasn't able to express my appreciation to my ex-wife for that, and this caused stress and tension in our postdivorce relationship.

I brought this up to my Inner Voice coach in late April. He listened and pointed out that Mother's Day was coming up in May. He suggested that I use that holiday to reach out to my ex-wife in a way that would show her how grateful I was for all the good things she had been and still was. He thought that if I did this, my warrior self would become much less tormenting and troublesome.

I took the advice, sending her a Mother's Day bouquet of flowers with a message that thanked her for being the wonderful mother she had been and still was to our sons. She accepted the flowers and my message gracefully. Now when we see each other at family gatherings, my warrior self rarely appears.

And whenever I'm in a difficult situation and feel tempted to head into battle, I have been able to apply this same strategy of dealing with my warrior self by demonstrating my recognition of others' positive attributes. I don't always send flowers, but I acknowledge the other person's good points. I do it clearly, openly, and in a way that I once thought would have made me vulnerable but that I've come to understand gives me more strength than I'd ever had before.

— Luke,

entrepreneur, investor

Religion, God, and Prayer—Oh My!

Did you ever notice that many of us don't take the time to pray until we are in trouble? Then it's, "God, if you'll just bail me out of this once, I promise . . ." And we make all kinds of promises that we rarely keep. That's what we call a classic foxhole prayer: when soldiers in foxholes who might not otherwise pray suddenly turn to God, sometimes just asking for help ("Get me out of this alive") and sometimes bargaining ("If you'll do this for me, I'll stop eating so much chocolate, I'll stop drinking, I'll go to church, I'll spend more time with my kids, whatever"). I think we've all done it at one time or another, and I certainly did it when I first arrived at the retreat. In fact, the first week or so I was in Hawaii, I was so distraught and confused that I resorted to praying every night— although I'm not sure that what I was doing was really praying; it was more like whining and pleading. It went something like this: "God, please help me. Help me get rid of this anger, this anxiety, and this horrible fear and doubt. God, tell me what you want me to do with my life. Why am I here on this earth? What's the point? I've made lots of money, and I've had tremendous business success. I've raised a family and had all the material success one could ask for. What do you want me to do now?"

When I asked questions, I expected answers. In my various businesses, if I wanted to know about revenue, how a particular advertising strategy was working, or how a specific negotiation was progressing, a quick e-mail or text to the executive in charge of that area would get me that information within minutes (and if what I wanted to know wasn't immediately available, a team would promptly begin working to do the necessary research and report back to me as soon as possible). If I didn't get a prompt response, I flexed my well-toned "expectation muscles" to make sure people knew not to keep me waiting. If I was curious about something outside my business, I would find someone who would teach me what I wanted to know and answer my questions. In fact, it wasn't unusual for me to hire people who could essentially tutor me in subjects that interested me. But this time, in spite of my heartfelt pleas for answers, none came. It was quite a blow to my ego, and it left me bewildered. But rather than making me angry, this silence from the universe prompted me to examine my relationship with the Creator.

When I was growing up, I attended a variety of churches. As an adult, attending church was important to me and to my wife as well. Our family attended a number of different churches as I tried to find a religious belief that would work for us. I believed that there was a God, the creator of the universe. Even so, while I believed in God, I never really knew Him. I didn't have a real relationship with God.

When I had business success, even though I credited my own abilities for it, I would usually remember to say, "Thanks, God, for whatever part you had in that. Now, when I get to the next deal, feel free to pitch in and help." I didn't mean any disrespect then, and I don't mean any disrespect now. That's just how it was. I thought I was responsible for what I accomplished, and I didn't figure God had much to do with it, but I was willing to give Him at least some credit. And I shared my success: over the years, I've donated millions of dollars to churches, temples, and religious or-ganizations (and plenty of secular charities as well). I wasn't trying to buy salvation or pay dues or impress anyone; I've just always believed that those of us who are blessed with material success should share.

I've studied the Bible for years, can quote scripture with the best, and believe that it provides excellent guidance for our lives. I've done the same with a long list of other religious books. But I was missing that personal contact with God. The more I learned, the more questions I had. Who is God, anyway? What does He look like? Does He talk? How do I know He really exists? Where's the proof?

Perhaps you already know those answers. When I was in Ha-waii, thousands of miles from home, I certainly didn't. My mar-riage had crumbled, and I'd lost control of my business along with a great deal of my net worth. I was feeling totally broken. But today I'm completely whole and confident. I've figured out some answers that make sense to me and have changed my life, and I'm going to share that knowledge with you.

Let me pause here to assure you that I'm not trying to convert you to any specific faith. As I've already said, this is not a religious book. It doesn't subscribe to any particular religion; rather, it subscribes to all of them. *Inner Voice* is about what I've learned about spirituality and getting connected to the God of your understanding, not about following any particular dogma—although it will still work for you, no matter what faith or creed you subscribe to. You'll see that as we go along.

So there I was in Hawaii, praying every day, asking what I was supposed to do with my life, and getting no answer. Gradually it dawned on me that this was nothing new. I don't think I'd ever really had a conversation where I felt I had received concrete answers from the God I knew from going to church, and if I did receive answers, I didn't know how to recognize the God voice. I prayed, I sent the words up—but it seemed as if nothing ever came down. I was frustrated, angry, and impatient. I wanted to know what I was supposed to do with the rest of my life—and I wanted to know now!

I shared my frustrations with the life coaches and spiritual counselors at the Hawaiian retreat. Of course, they told me to be patient, and they worked with me on that and other issues. I knew I was making progress; it just wasn't happening fast enough to suit me. Then one day, Herman, the fellow who had met me at the airport when I first landed in Hawaii (and who has since become a close personal friend), gave me a simple bit of advice that was the beginning of a huge breakthrough to my own inner voice.

My problem with prayer, Herman told me, was that I had God on the outside and not on the inside. "Russ, once you get God on the inside, it will move you to a much higher and closer contact with Him," he told me.

I'd like to be able to say that bells rang, lights flashed, and I had a clear vision of my future, but that's not the way it was. I just looked at Herman and tried to process his words. I didn't really understand what he meant. I had to get God on the inside? How was I supposed to do that? I kept thinking about it throughout the day. That night, I prayed my usual prayer, asking God to help me get over my anger, frustration, fear, and doubt. I asked Him to please let me know what I was supposed to do for this second half of my life. And then, remembering what Herman had said, I went a step further. I asked God to come on the inside.

I said those words out loud, and as I did, I pointed at my mouth, my nose, and my ears. Why? Because they are all openings to the inside of my body. Hilarious, right? Not really. It shows how desperate I was. And I ended my prayer that night by saying, "God, I don't quite know what Herman is talking about, but if You're supposed to come inside me, then come on!"

And nothing happened again—until the next day, when I had what I now understand was my first Inner Voice Awakening. For the first time, I consciously received direction from a power greater than myself. That's a long story that I'll share with you later, when I show you how you can achieve clear contact with your inner voice. For now, what's important is that I opened up, let my guard down, and let the thoughts (God) in. It wasn't an earthshattering experience, but it was progress.

What Does God Look Like?

Do you have some sort of mental image of God? I don't know what God looks like, but I think I'm safe in saying that He's not some bearded old guy in a flowing robe who floats around in the sky making notes of when we've been good and bad (that would be Santa Claus, right?). I believe God doesn't have to keep score, because our universe has a clear, recognizable structure that pretty much does all the scorekeeping itself. The building blocks of that structure are what I call "immutable laws of the universe." Essentially, those immutable laws are the rules that God (or the universe or whatever you call the creator) has put in place for the order of human life that we must live by. While we do have a significant degree of power and control in our lives, we can't change an immutable law. *Immutable* means unchangeable, irreversible, absolute, undeniable. Immutable laws are designed to guide your life, so it makes sense for you to understand them. There's no point in resisting. In fact, fighting immutable laws is like trying to teach a pig to sing: It only wastes your time and annoys the pig.

Here's an example of an immutable law: You can't plant a pumpkin seed and get a thornbush. It just can't happen. And if you plant an acorn, it will—in time and with the proper care—grow into a tall oak tree. It will never grow into a palm tree. Why is that? Because that's the way the universe is organized; it simply is—it's an immutable law. You'll always get what you plant, so plant the seeds you want to harvest.

When we are in the warrior phase of life, we waste a lot of time fighting immutable laws.

Inner Voice Whispers

Step back from your disappointment and reconnect with your passion. Know that there is a positive and effective way forward.

As we grow into the statesperson phase, we understand them, accept them, and learn to make them work for us.

Experience, Strength, and Hope

One of the beautiful aspects of the Inner Voice way of life is that it's a program based on suggestions. We don't tell others what to do. We don't give advice or opinions, we simply offer suggestions based on our own experience. If we don't have the appropriate experience, we either say nothing or turn to another member of the Inner Voice community for help.

It works like this: If you come to me with an issue you're struggling with and I have some experience with that issue, I'll share it.

I'll tell you what I learned about the way to handle the situation that made me stronger and what I did that made my life better and gave me continued hope. What you do from that point is entirely your decision.

This is very different from what I did in warrior mode. As a warrior, when someone came to me for advice, I was quick to say things like, "You should do this . . ." and "You ought to do that . . ." and I expected my advice to be followed. Now, at the risk of sounding like a warrior, my advice was usually sound, but that's not the point. The point is that my advice was more of a command. As a statesperson, I want to help others by sharing experience, strength, and hope—and then letting people make their own decisions with the guidance of the inner voice.

Inner Voice Whispers

You don't need anyone's permission to live a successful, happy life filled with exactly what you see in your dreams. You don't need to wish, beg, or plead for a lucky break. You just have to step forward and do it.

Here's something else that I've come to understand about the Inner Voice way of life: What we think we're doing for others we're really doing for ourselves. We'll always receive a greater benefit from our positive, statesperson actions than anyone else does, as long as we act consistently within Inner Voice principles. I can't count the number of times I've coached someone in which I had an opportunity to share my experience, strength, and hope, and, as a result, this process of sharing provided me with information or perspective that I needed to deal with something in my own life. More often than not, I get an even greater benefit than the person I'm trying to help. It's a wonderful way to live. Even something as simple as common courtesy benefits us far more than it does the person we hold the door for. In a very special way, the Inner Voice way of life is one of the most selfish—and consequently most rewarding—ways of life you can choose.

Connecting the Dots

Sometimes the events of our lives don't make sense until we're forced to come to terms with our own mortality. The late Steve Jobs talked about this several years ago in a commencement speech he gave at Stanford University. At the time, he had survived his first bout with cancer and had engaged in the type of introspection that often accompanies a serious illness. Although Jobs didn't use this specific language, his message is that what we do and what happens to us as a result aren't coincidence but unconscious contact with the inner voice. If you've never heard this speech, I urge you to go to YouTube and watch it.

Jobs was adopted as an infant by blue-collar parents who promised his birth mother that they would send him to college—and they were willing to spend their life savings to keep that promise. But he didn't see much benefit in college and, not wanting to exhaust his parents' savings, dropped out after the first six months. He hung around the school for another 18 months, sleeping on the floor of friends' dorm rooms and dropping in on courses that interested him. One of those courses was a calligraphy class. He was fascinated with the history and creativity of typography. Ten years later, while he and Steve Wozniak were designing the Macintosh computer in his parents' garage, Jobs included different fonts with the proper spacing so that users could design beautiful computer-generated documents, a feature that made the Mac the computer of choice for graphic designers and that's now standard for all operating systems.

Had Jobs been adopted by parents who had more money, he might never have dropped out of college and sat in on that calligraphy course—and computers might look very different than they do today. But the point Jobs makes and that we all need to understand is the importance of connecting the dots backward, of taking the time to understand how we got to where we are so that we can forge the right path into the future.

All of our experiences—the good and the bad, the seemingly minor and clearly major—help us determine our purpose and passion for ourselves. They provide direction. And, if we learn to use them, they give us the knowledge and wisdom we need to achieve our purpose.

When I look back at my life and connect the dots, I can see that I was always in the plan God had for me; I just didn't know it then. And I can tell you confidently that you are, too. Wherever you are is where you're supposed to be, and where you're supposed to be today is not where you're meant to stay.

So, how do you find out the plan for your life and the purpose you were put here to accomplish and, in that process, move from warrior to statesperson? I've developed a tool called the Discovery Chart that will guide you through the process of connecting the dots backward so that you can see how your life's plan has unfolded and then build the foundation you need to move forward.

Visualize one of the connect-the-dots drawing puzzles you probably completed as a child. Until you begin marking a solid line between the dots, it looks like just a jumble of random dots and numbers. But when you connect those dots, a clear picture emerges. You can do that same exercise metaphorically with your life.

There are a couple of ways to connect the dots backward. You can start at the present and trace it back to the beginning to see how you got to today. Or you can go back to the beginning and move forward, looking at how things fit together, how certain incidents affected you and your life. That's what I did. I used the Discovery Chart to connect the dots of my early childhood, my teen years, and my young adulthood to clearly see the picture that's me today.

The most important thing to remember when it comes to seeing the big picture of our lives is that we can only connect the dots backward because it's impossible to connect them forward.

We know what has already happened, but we don't know what *will* happen.

You can see a blank chart in the "Inner Voice Charts" section at the back of the book. In Chapters 5 and 6, I'll explain how the Discovery Chart will help you understand what drives you, help you progress from warrior to statesperson, and walk you through the process of doing it. Keep in mind that we don't have to solidly and permanently be in one phase or the other; we can move back and forth or be somewhere in between. When you evolve to statesperson, you'll meet your soul self (a concept I'll explain later). Once you do that, you never have to go back unless you make the conscious decision to do so.

Connecting the dots backward using the Discovery Chart will help you see the plan for your life and give you plenty of evidence to prove it. When you understand that, you'll naturally stop resisting, you'll experience instant relief, and you'll see life start falling into place as the creator meant it to do.

Something else the Discovery Chart will do is help you let go of the past and learn to live in the present—which is the only place you need to be. Let's talk about why that's so important.

CHAPTER THREE

ALL YOU NEED IS NOW

We are not promised tomorrow.

This is important. It's the foundation of living the Inner Voice way of life.

In all my travels and studies, working with spiritual and religious leaders from all walks of life and faiths, they all agree that while we may be promised many things, we are not promised a tomorrow. God didn't build human beings with enough energy for tomorrow, next week, or next year. We were only built with enough energy for today.

I've also learned that we need to let go of the past. Hanging on to the past takes a huge amount of energy; and just as we don't have enough energy for tomorrow, we also don't have enough energy for yesterday. We do, however, have enough for today, and that's all we need.

This is one of the most meaningful Inner Voice concepts. As simple and logical as it is, it's still hard to let go of the past and not worry about the future. This isn't something we learn to do that automatically becomes second nature, like walking or riding a bicycle. Living in today is something we must practice doing every day. Even as well as I understand this, I still occasionally find myself trying to live where I'm not supposed to be, either in the past or the future. I recognize what I'm doing when I start feeling anger, anxiety, frustration, fear, doubt, guilt, and shame—all emotions that we aren't meant to live in.

So what should you do when those negative emotions start dragging you to a place you don't need to go? Practice humility, powerlessness, and surrender. As you learn these techniques for staying in the present, you'll see that they often overlap. One leads to another; understanding one helps clarify another. Being humble takes our focus away from ourselves and puts it onto others in a positive way. Understanding and accepting when we are powerless helps us to stop wasting energy trying to manage and control what we can't. And when we surrender the issues and feelings that are keeping us from being happy, joyous, and spiritually free, we take ourselves to the place and time where we're meant to be, which is now.

Inner Voice
Whispers

When you spend your time stuck in yesterday or trying to live in tomorrow, you create a block to your inner voice.

Humility Is Something We Learn to Do, Not Define

One of the many things that stood out about all the people at the retreat in Hawaii was that they were all so very nice and seemed to have an inner peace that I wasn't ready to trust at first. They were thoughtful and considerate, always putting others first. It went beyond mere good manners, beyond superficial courtesy. It was something I'd never seen in a group before, and I didn't immediately understand it. I wasn't sure exactly what it was or how to get it, but I remember saying to myself, "Whatever this peace is that these people have, I want it. If I don't learn anything else during my time here but can leave with that peace, kindness, tolerance, and patience, it will be worth every bit of time, every bit of money, and every bit of crisis I've been through to get here."

I finally figured out that what I was seeing was genuine humility. I've learned that true humility goes beyond just being humble and modest. The word *humility* also means grounded, and the concept addresses intrinsic self-worth. Humility gives us the firmest possible foundation for building genuine self-confidence, because it lets us see ourselves in a greater context. Humility is multidimensional; it includes self-understanding, awareness, and openness. It's a virtue extolled in all major religions. Some of the world's greatest leaders and teachers have consistently demonstrated humility.

I always thought that the humility and the extreme kindness I saw among the staff at the retreat were a weakness. If you weren't tough and hard, you would get taken advantage of. If you weren't strong, cocky, confident, and in charge, you couldn't be a successful leader. I now know that this is just warrior thinking. As a practicing statesperson, I've come to understand that true humility takes tremendous strength. Being genuinely humble means we don't have to pretend, don't have to worry about being good enough, because we have accepted who we are and are confident in our place in the world. This is why I often say that humility isn't something we merely define; it's something we learn how to do. Practicing humility requires action.

To "do" humility, we must learn to serve others honestly, even as we seek the direction of the God of our individual understanding in working on our own issues. When I'm in warrior phase, I'm often a "fixer." I like to help people. That's a good thing, but it doesn't involve humility if I'm trying to control others. For me, learning to "do" humility meant accepting that I'm not in charge of how others feel or what they do. I'm only in charge of keeping my side of the fence clean and doing what God is telling me to do. There's no time when I'm freer and more at peace than when I'm actively practicing true humility by serving others without any attempt to control them or anything else over which I am powerless.

Powerlessness Is Powerful

Before my journey of self-discovery began, I thought I understood power. I thought it was being in charge, owning, and controlling. I thought that by the sheer force of my own will, I could
make things go the way I wanted—and often I did. It's possible
to exercise power in other ways. Some people manipulate others
by being negative. Others do it through gossip, finger-pointing,
and blaming. Any negative human characteristic can be used to
try to exert power, control, or manipulation. Although it might
work sometimes, it's not an effective long-term life strategy. And
it causes a level of stress that can seriously damage your relationships and your health.

In Hawaii, I learned that we are powerless over other people,
many day-to-day happenings, and other situations in our lives.
When we try to control or manipulate the outcomes of the things
over which we are powerless, our own lives become unmanageable. We become frustrated, depressed, and angry and experience
a host of other negative emotions. Our relationships suffer because we waste so much energy trying to solve the unsolvable. We
don't want to admit that we lack control over other people and
most situations, because we believe it's a sign of weakness. Yet in
accepting our powerlessness, we actually gain control of our lives
in all the areas that matter.

So how do we deal with powerlessness? By surrendering.

Surrender to Win

When I arrived in Hawaii, the drive from the airport to the
retreat gave Herman an opportunity to introduce me to some concepts that were foreign to me. One thing he said was that for me
to get the most out of my time there, I would need to understand
and practice the principle of surrender.

Surrender? Me? You don't know who Russ Whitney is, I thought. *I
don't give up. I fight to the end.* I remember that he talked more
about this foreign concept, but I don't recall specifically what he

34

said then. As with many of the Inner Voice principles I would hear over the next several months and years, understanding would take time.

As I grappled with the concepts of humility and powerless-ness, my new role models on this first leg of my journey gave me even more to think about. They told me that what we have to do to win over powerlessness is surrender. They had to use the win-lose language for me to understand, because my per-ception was that people who surrendered were losers and I was (I thought) a winner.

Surrender can be a scary word, especially for a warrior. I used to think that surrender meant admitting defeat, quit-ting, or letting someone else have the power and control that was rightfully mine. That was more warrior thinking— and once I understood that, I was able to understand this: Surrender doesn't mean quitting; it means winning. It doesn't mean you're not in charge; it means you have a new and improved way to take charge without fighting everything and everyone.

Inner Voice Whispers

Be in the moment.
Let life flow, and things
will fall into place.
Stay out of tomorrow
and don't bring yesterday
into today.

It's only after we learn what surrender is and how to put it into action, and then see the result, that we can understand its immense power and strength.

How do you learn to surrender? To begin with, it's important for you to know that there are two parts to surrender. The first is the obvious: Turn the issue over to God. Give it up. Let it go. The second—which is often overlooked—is to listen for God to give you an answer or direction. When you're able to do both, you have made great progress in achieving and maintaining consis-tent, conscious contact with God. This takes practice.

Often when you surrender an issue that you have with what someone else is doing, you'll hear God telling you to change your own behavior. That's happened to me more times than I like to admit. Even while I was working on this book, I had an issue with a couple of family members who weren't behaving as I thought they should. When I surrendered the situation, God clearly told me that He was in control, that those family members where were they needed to be, and that I needed to let them move at their own pace; and then God told me to do something for someone else (a specific person and situation). I listened, I understood, I acted—and I found peace. When you surrender, God will give you an action strategy.

Let me share with you how I learned surrender the first time. You can do it the way I did, or you can come up with your own strategy.

When I started listening to the coaches and life experts in Hawaii, I began hearing a lot of ideas that were new to me—or at least that I hadn't paid much attention to before. I wasn't convinced about this whole surrender idea—I was, after all, still a warrior—but I decided to give it a try. So at the end of each day, just before going to bed, I got on my knees and talked to the God of my understanding about the problems that were bothering me. And I gave Him my problems. My side of the conversation would typically go something like this: "God, this situation is causing me to be angry, and I know I'm not supposed to have that. You clearly say that if anything is causing me anger, anxiety, frustration, fear, or doubt, I'm supposed to give that to You, and You'll handle it for me. So, here it is. Here's my problem, and I'm not going to worry about it anymore. It's Yours." Then I would get into bed and go to sleep.

Now, I don't know that there are any rules that say you have to get on your knees to surrender. The reason I did it that way in the beginning was that it forced me to practice humility as well. Remember, humility is something we do. By getting on my knees, I was humbling myself to my creator. I also did it only at night, because I thought it was arrogant to assume that the creator of the universe was going to be available to me "on demand." Today I know better: I can surrender at any time during the day or night—in any posture, in any place—and the creator is ready to take my problems and tell me what, if anything, I need to do. But I had to start somewhere, so I started on my knees.

Remember, letting go of the issue—turning it over to God—is just the first part of surrender. If something is enough of a problem for you to need surrender, it's enough of a problem for you to completely surrender, which means listening for an answer after you've turned it over. How do you do that? You take a break from whatever you're doing and clear your mind of clutter so that you can hear the answer. I like to go for a bike ride; I find that being outside and getting some great exercise is a perfect time to quiet my thoughts and wait for an answer to what I've surrendered. You could also go for a walk or a run. If you're in the car, turn off the radio. Or you could simply move to a quiet place with no distractions. Noninterruption is the key to getting a clear Inner Voice surrender message.

How to know whether the answer is truly coming from God or some other source is something I would learn later, and I'll share that with you when I explain how to have two-way conscious contact with the creator.

You may not get an answer right away, but you still need to listen. Taking the time to step away from the noise of the day is an important part of the process. You may need some space between the time you surrender and the time the answer comes. Sometimes the answer will tell you what you need to do—and sometimes the answer is that the situation is resolved without any further action on your part. And if you find yourself continuing to dwell on the problem, trying to come up with solutions on your own, you haven't completely surrendered; keep working on letting go.

There's no issue too small or too large for surrender. Make it a habit. Every night before I get into bed, I surrender anything that's causing me anger, anxiety, frustration, fear, doubt, guilt, or shame. Then I wait for the answer to come in the morning. Sometimes the answer is what I need to do; sometimes the answer is that I don't have to do anything. It's human nature to think that we always have to do something, that God will tell us and we must act. The truth is that sometimes God doesn't want us to do anything; He wants us to have faith and let Him handle it. So surrender and listen, knowing that sometimes what you're going to hear is, "I'm glad you turned this over to Me. I'll take care of it."

LIVING THE INNER VOICE LIFE

I Knew He Was the One—Why Didn't He?

After spending much of my adult life in one failed relationship after another, I found my soul mate. Shortly after we began dating, I was introduced to the Inner Voice program. Two years later, I was more than ready to get married, but my boyfriend was ignoring my hints.

Upset and frustrated, I talked to my Inner Voice coach. He explained that I couldn't control my boyfriend, that I couldn't make him propose. I needed to surrender it. I used the program strategies and surrendered—and felt immediate relief from the stress and anxiety I had been experiencing.

A few weeks later, my boyfriend wanted to go ring shopping. Not long after that, he proposed at an amusement park by having a caricaturist draw us together with "Will you marry me?" across the top.

We are now happily married, and I have no doubt it was because I practiced the Inner Voice principle of surrender.

— Nancy,
education management

Surrender in Action

For many years, I owned a construction company with three partners. At one point, the company had reached more than $700 million in sales. After the real estate bubble burst, we decided to close the company. The two operating partners—who had been friends of mine for more than 20 years—shut the office down; took all of the desks, computers, and other office equipment; and opened up another office. They never called a meeting to discuss what they were doing; they just wound things down, helped themselves to what was left, and moved on. I didn't even know what they were doing until the fourth partner discovered it and called me one evening. We were both pretty worked up about it. I was feeling betrayed and angry, and I decided to call my lawyer and begin legal action the next day.

As I continued to stew about the situation that evening, I realized the alarm bells for surrender were going off. I was feeling anger, anxiety, frustration, fear, and doubt. But even as my warrior training was telling me to go into battle, I knew that I had to surrender. I went to my knees that night and said, "God, I know suing and vengeance aren't from You. I'm not supposed to have this anger, fear, and doubt. But I feel like I'm being cheated! I know that when I feel like this, I'm supposed to surrender it to You. So here it is!"

As I mentioned, one of the ways in which I meditate and get ready to listen to answers is to take my bicycle out for a long ride. One of the many benefits of living in Florida is that I can do

Inner Voice Whispers

If you want to feel more positive, more empowered, more confident, and more encouraged, be useful. Making a difference for others makes a big difference for you.

that year-round. It's a way that I can get out into nature without phones or other distractions. If I can't get out on my bike, I either take a walk or just go to a quiet place first thing in the morning so that I can clear my head and listen. After I had surrendered this business issue the night before, I went for a bike ride early the next day and rode for about an hour. I was almost home without any answers, and I was starting to feel a little anxious.

Then I got the message. A clear thought popped into my head: *Call your accountant and ask him to do a closing audit on the company. Call your partners and politely ask if they would agree that it's a good idea to audit the company to be sure the books are in order and all the taxes are paid. Don't make any accusations or threats.*

The peace that came over me at that moment was unbelievable. It was such a simple solution to an issue that was causing me such angst. You would think that as a businessperson with plenty of experience in starting, growing, selling, and even closing down companies, I would have thought of it right away. But I didn't— and I know for sure that the idea didn't come from my human self. It came to me through my inner voice.

I followed the direction and called my three partners. They all agreed that it was a smart idea and that we should do it. They even asked if I could arrange for my accountant to handle it.

My accountant thought it was a good idea, too. Within an hour after the audit team showed up, they found a check payable to me for $185,000 in the desk drawer of one of the operating partners. It was dated about six months earlier. The partner wasn't trying to cheat me; it was an oversight. And we were making so much money at the time, before the real estate bubble burst, that I hadn't noticed not receiving the payment.

The accountants told us that everything was in good order and that we could proceed with shutting the company down. They also told me that it was customary for the operating partners to take the furnishings and equipment if they wanted it, because it was already depreciated and didn't have much value.

What could have turned into a huge legal battle that would have cost friendships and money was settled in one day for a comparatively nominal amount due to the power of surrender—and I got a $185,000 bonus!

The real bottom line is this: Anything that causes you anger, anxiety, frustration, fear, doubt, guilt, or shame should be immediately surrendered. Then sit back, get quiet, and listen for answers. They will come.

LIVING THE INNER VOICE LIFE

Letting Go of a Good Deal Got Me a Great Deal

My wife and I had sold our home and found a new home that we loved. As so often happens in real estate transactions, the timing wasn't precise; we had to be out of our old home ten days before we could close on the new one. We decided to take advantage of that time to enjoy a vacation at the beach with our three children.

The day after we closed on the sale of our old home, the seller of the beautiful condominium we were contracted to buy backed out of the deal. So there I was, a successful businessperson with a family, essentially homeless. I did everything humanly possible to contact the seller to persuade him to honor the deal, but I couldn't get through to him. He wouldn't return my texts, e-mails, or calls, and all his real estate agent would say was that he was canceling the sale.

I was going crazy and thinking about suing the seller. All of my family's belongings were in short-term storage, and we were staying at a hotel. It had taken us months to find this place, and the idea of staying in a hotel for an extended period while we looked for a new home that would suit us as well as this one did was extremely distressing.

41

LIVING THE INNER VOICE LIFE, CONT.

My Inner Voice coach had recently introduced me to the concept of surrender—something that wasn't easy for a hard-charging, in-control guy like me to grasp. When I called my coach and told him what was happening, he advised me to forget about suing and to surrender the situation. Easy for him to say! It took me two full days to completely surrender, but when I did, the sense of freedom and peace was amazing. I took my kids to the hotel pool to enjoy a swim, and while we were there, I struck up a conversation with some other guests. During the course of our small talk, we figured out that one of the men was the seller who had just backed out of the deal that had left me and my family homeless.

Wow! We marveled at the incredible odds that the two of us should end up not only staying at the same hotel, but also around the pool at the same time, in close enough proximity to begin talking to each other. Even as I thought, *What an amazing coincidence,* I remembered what I had been taught about coincidence: that when things like this happen, they're not coincidence; they're part of a larger plan. We were obviously meant to meet, but why?

I said, "I can understand that you changed your mind about selling, but why wouldn't you return any of my calls or e-mails?"

"My attorney told me not to," he said.

I wanted to punch him, but I could hear my Inner Voice coach (or maybe it was my inner voice) saying, "Surrender! Surrender!" So instead of resorting to violence, I calmly told him about the stress he had caused my family: how we had sold our previous home and now had to find a new place to live.

LIVING THE INNER VOICE LIFE, CONT.

He told me that he had a friend in the same complex who owned a condo that was nicer than his that was going to be on the market soon. We met with the real estate agent and struck a great deal on his friend's condo, and the real estate agent helped us find a short-term rental in the condo complex where we could stay until we closed on the new deal. Because I surrendered instead of fighting, I was able to buy a condo we liked better at a lower price.

Learning to surrender has changed my life. It has become my automatic response when I'm faced with a situation over which I am powerless.

— Alec,
entrepreneur

If It Worked for Me, Can it Work for You?

Surrender works for anything that's causing anger, frustration, and discord in your life, not just things related to business and money. For example, I was in an up-and-down relationship for several years. She was a wonderful woman, but we had a destructive pattern of breaking up and getting back together over and over. In hindsight, I can see that I kept going back to the relationship for all the wrong reasons: I didn't want to fail, and I didn't want to see her with another man. Finally, I realized I was powerless over the relationship, and I surrendered it. I asked God to help me get over the resentment and to give me guidance. I heard the answer clearly; God said, "Russ, she is also My child, and I love her as much as I love you. I have other plans for her. Let her go. Give her back to Me."

With that answer, I was finally able to have peace with the ending of the relationship so that we could both move on and pursue our own individual purposes. I still care about her, of course, but I understand that God has other plans for each of us. I had to get quiet enough and have enough faith in the Inner Voice principles to surrender and hear the plan. Had I not surrendered, we'd probably still be in that vicious cycle of breaking up and making up, and neither one of us would be truly happy.

Surrender is a principle that comes up regularly when I'm coaching. Here's an example: Andrew is a good friend and client I've been personally coaching on the Inner Voice principles and strategies. He's a former professional rugby player from Australia, about six feet tall, 260 pounds, and as tough as they come. Although he is a multimillionaire who has been very successful in business, he has embraced the Inner Voice program, because he knew something was missing in his life.

Inner Voice
Whispers

Be grateful first thing in the morning. Find the good in everything all day long. If you don't have something positive to say, say nothing.

Andrew and his brother, Eric, who still lives in Australia, have a business. Andrew called me because he and Eric were having a serious dispute over a business issue. They had been fighting over money, territory, and ego for months. Andrew was beside himself because they were no longer speaking and, instead, were threatening to sue each other.

I listened to the details and asked Andrew if he wanted a suggestion. When he said yes, I took the time to lay a foundation for what I thought he should do. I said, "I'm offering this suggestion based on what I've been taught by great leaders who are far more advanced than I am. I'll pass on to you what they've passed on to me. For me, this approach has been wildly successful. But let me prepare you now; this may not be the advice you're looking for."

I paused to give him an opportunity to change his mind about hearing what I had to say.

"Russ, I trust you," he said. "You've been a great friend and coach for me and my family, and you've helped us more than you know. Right now, I'm feeling very vengeful and I want to attack, but I'm open to your ideas."

He had asked for my opinion and agreed to listen, so I continued. "Andrew, I'm not telling you what to do; I'm telling you what I've done. I've been in business disputes with people I cared deeply about, and it's always worked out best when I've put the relationship first. If it were me, I'd call my brother tonight. Better yet, use Skype so that you can see each other. But before you begin, invite God into the call and have the discussion as if God were there, in person, on the line with you—because He is. Start the call by telling Eric that you love him, that you're sorry for your part in this whole dispute, and that you want to work it out. Tell him that he's your brother and there's no amount of money, no business disagreement worth losing a brother over. Ask him if he will think about the differences you have and if he will then offer up a solution that could work for both of you. Then surrender the whole thing to God."

Andrew's response wasn't surprising. "What? Are you crazy? No way would I ever do that. I'm in the right, this is crap, and I'm not putting myself in a position of weakness like that."

"Well, you asked for my input, and that's what it is," I said mildly. "What you decide to do is up to you." After a few more minutes, we ended the call.

The next evening, Andrew called and essentially said, "Do you have any other suggestions?" I think Andrew was figuring that I would have a different answer after having had a day to consider his options. Or maybe he knew this was right but was looking for more reassurance before he accepted it. In any case, I told him the same thing: "Tell your brother you love him, and ask him to come up with the solution." And again, he rejected the suggestion—although not quite as forcefully.

When Andrew called me the following night, we discussed the situation for the third time. This time, he reluctantly agreed to call his brother. He admitted that all of the other Inner Voice suggestions I'd given him during our coaching had worked wonderfully; so even though he was resistant, he would give this one a try.

The result was amazing. Andrew did exactly as I had suggested: He Skyped Eric and told him that he loved him, that no business deal was worth losing a brother over, and that he wanted Eric to come up with a resolution to their conflict. They both laughed and cried, and apologized to each other—these two big, strong warrior men. They agreed to work it out. Within a few days, the difference was resolved, and they both walked away from the deal with several million dollars.

I confess that when I was in my warrior stage, I would never have done anything like what I advised Andrew to do. I would have been determined to win at any cost—and it would have been a protracted, painful, expensive battle. And that's what Andrew wanted to do before he agreed to try the Inner Voice principle of surrender.

What about you? Is there anything going on in your life that you could surrender today? Could practicing humility, admitting powerlessness, and surrendering whatever is troubling you let you triumph over the situation? For me, the answer is absolutely yes. And it's all in how you play the game of life.

CHAPTER FOUR

THE GAME OF LIFE

In my search for the meaning of life, I've come to understand that life is essentially a game that consists of a daily search for the truth with the creator of your understanding. When you realize this, it gets easier to live in the present. If you think about professional sports, this makes sense: The players prepare for the game, play it, learn from it, and then play the next one. They don't spend a lot of time beating themselves up over something they did that they can't do over. They don't spend a lot of time worrying about the next game; they understand the difference between preparation and worry. When they are playing the game, that's all they're focused on: playing the game right now. And that's what you should focus on: playing the game of life right now in the here and now—that is, today!

Inner Voice Whispers

The greatest achievement was first a thought. The mighty oak sleeps in the acorn. If you have a dream, it is the seedling of a reality. You wouldn't have the thought if you couldn't fulfill the dream.

The Time Clock of Life

The game of life is a lot like any game that's played under a time clock. For example, in a basketball or football game, there are

60 minutes on the clock. The game starts, it's played for an hour, and then it ends. It's done. The scoreboard tells you whether you won or lost. And regardless of how you did in that game, you go on to the next one and the score starts over at zero.

In life, each "game" is one day. Today. Our season—instead of being a period of months, as in sports—is our lives. But if you ask professional athletes if they spend any time or energy while they're on the field or the court thinking about the last game or their next game, they'll most likely tell you no. They are focused on the now, on the game they're playing at the moment. That's how winning seasons are achieved and championships are won: one day at a time, one game at a time.

> *Inner Voice Whispers*
>
> Resentments bond you to the past and keep the flow of ideas and positivity from getting in. Forgive and get on with your life.

This isn't to say that players don't train; they absolutely do. They practice, they study their opponents, and they develop their skills. They have strategies to reach their goals. But when they're "in the game," that's the only place where they are. When they get "out of the game," when they are distracted even for a moment, is when they make mistakes. They know it, and that's why they exercise the discipline to stay entirely in the present, in the game, while they're playing.

Of course, the "game of life" isn't about scoring baskets or touchdowns. As I've said, it's a daily search for the truth with you and the God of your understanding. A key word there is *daily;* the time clock is today. That doesn't mean that we can't have plans and goals for tomorrow, next week, and next year. We can, and we should. We just can't live in those goals; we have to stay in today. If we don't, we fall into anger, anxiety, frustration, fear, and doubt. We start to play the "what if" game: "What if this happens?" "What if that happens?" "What if I don't have enough money?" "What if I get sick, have an accident, or experience some other crisis?" Play that game, and you'll be filled with unnecessary anxiety. When you worry, you're essentially planning for bad things to happen. The way to avoid worry is to stay in the present. Today all is well, and you know what you have to do today. Keep it there.

If God didn't build us with enough energy to be in tomorrow, He certainly didn't give us enough energy for yesterday. Usually when we go into yesterday, we go into guilt, shame, and resentments. Certainly we all have happy memories, and we should treasure them. But most of the time, when we go back to yesterday, we waste a lot of time beating ourselves up about things we can't change. We focus on mistakes and regrets. That's time off today's clock.

A key question is this: When you're playing the game of life, how do you know if you're winning or losing? It's actually easy, because although the game of life isn't about scoring points, we still have a way to keep score.

Game of Life = Search for the truth

Time Clock of Life = Today

Scoreboard of Life = The ratio of the time you're happy, joyful, and free in spirit against the time you're feeling anger, anxiety, frustration, fear, doubt, guilt, and shame.

The Scoreboard of Life

If the game of life is a search for the truth and the time clock of life is today, you need a scoreboard to determine if you're winning or losing. Your scoreboard doesn't count points. Instead, it's a ratio that measures how happy, joyful, and spiritually free you are against your feelings of anger, anxiety, frustration, fear, doubt, guilt, and shame.

I May Be the Father, but I Didn't Know Best

After my divorce, my relationship with my then-teenage sons began to deteriorate. I did what I thought I was supposed to do for both of them: in addition to providing financial support, I used my connections to help them find jobs, continue their education, and have a place to live and transportation. Still, they foundered, unable to hold jobs, and one dropped out of high school and got into serious trouble. We eventually became estranged and didn't communicate for years. My "business self" wanted to believe that my sons were lost causes, getting what they deserved. Maybe they were, but that wasn't making me feel any better. I loved them, missed them, and felt the pain of our relationship—or lack of one—every day.

Then I was introduced to the Inner Voice. My life in general and my relationship with my sons in particular began to change dramatically.

I learned how the application of a few simple principles could reveal the source of what was causing my chronic discomfort with what had become a wholly dysfunctional body of relationships. My true *aha* moment (the first realization of what my inner voice had been trying to tell me) was when I finally grasped that I couldn't change what had happened and that the way I'd been doing things obviously wasn't getting me where I wanted to be. I applied the Inner Voice principles and received an answer that worked immediately, effectively, and in an amazingly rewarding way.

LIVING THE INNER VOICE LIFE, CONT.

Today, my relationship with my now-adult sons is the best it's ever been. I'm close to them both. In fact, I've introduced the Inner Voice way of life to my older son. He applied what he learned, and his professional life has taken a totally new direction to a vocation that has been his passion since he was a teenager (who knew?). More important is that he now has a 100 percent positive outlook on life in general.

Inner Voice principles showed me the path to a new and highly gratifying way of addressing my relationships; all I had to do was learn how to listen.

— Lawrence,
corporate finance consultant

As I've said, I don't believe our creator is some judgmental creature floating around in the sky, looking like Moses and keeping score on us. Your inner voice gives you the gift of keeping score for yourself, and you get a new scoreboard every day. The happier and more spiritually free you are, the higher your score.

The Most Important Rules of the Game

In the early days of my journey to discover the inner voice, I learned some simple words of wisdom. Some call it a *prayer*, some prefer to call it a *mantra*; it doesn't matter what term you use. What's important is that you understand it.

Grant me the serenity to accept the things I cannot change,
Give me the courage to change the things I can,
And give me the wisdom to know the difference.

Let's break this down so that you can see how to use it and how it ties in with mastering the game of life:

Grant me the serenity to accept the things I cannot change.

A grant is a gift. By saying this prayer, I'm asking my creator for a gift: the gift of serenity, which means peace. But I'm not asking for serenity in general; I'm asking for God to give me the gift of being able to accept peacefully and calmly the things I can't change.

I can't change yesterday. I can't change who I was or any of my past behaviors. I can't change who raised me. I can't change that I have probably offended people, missed a meeting, or made some bad choices. I can't change any of the things in my past that I'm not proud of. I can't change any of the things I wish I hadn't done or at least had done differently.

What I can do is practice forgiveness, forgiveness of others and of myself. I can admit that the past is what it is. But as I do that, I also recognize that the past doesn't have to be who I am today. This is one of the most amazing gifts that God gives us: the power to forgive ourselves and be at peace with the past. No one and no creator ever holds that back from us; all we have to do is accept it and use it. You are the only one who has the power to either continue to punish yourself for something you can't change, or forgive yourself and move on. We often find forgiving ourselves extremely difficult, often more so than forgiving others. The Inner Voice principles help you deal with this and learn to forgive yourself.

In addition to not being able to change the past, we also can't change other people. I can't tell you how many times I've shared the Inner Voice concept with people who've said, "Wow, I know someone who needs this!" I understand that because I've felt that way. Especially in the beginning, as I was first learning this, I was so excited that I wanted everyone to know about it. But people come to self-awareness and an understanding of the inner voice in their own time, in God's time. So when people say they know someone who needs the Inner Voice program, my response is, "I hope you're talking about yourself needing it, because we can't force this on others and we don't try. We share our experience, strength, and hope, and let others make their own decisions." The only person who can change a person is that person. Just as no one else can change you, you can't change anyone else. Let the inner voice help you accept and be at peace with that.

Give me the courage to change the things I can

The one thing I can change is me. But change isn't easy, and for many of us, it's downright frightening. It takes courage. And not every change we want to make will stick the first time we try it. That's why we must understand the time clock of life and live only in today. I can do anything for just one day. When I think about what I can change today, I think about this:

Today, I can have humility.
Today, I can have more patience.
Today, I can be kind.
Today, I can forgive and get over past resentments.
Today, I can apologize for something I did.
Today, I can make better decisions.
Today, I can be the person I want to be, because I have made a conscious decision to change.

And give me the wisdom to know the difference.

The wisdom to know the difference is the part that used to confuse the heck out of me; it's the part that's really hard to get when you're in the warrior phase. As a warrior, I understood (at least intellectually) that there were things I couldn't change, and if it was something that didn't really matter to me, I could easily accept it. But when warriors want to change something over which they have no power, they often don't realize that they're trying to change something they can't change; they don't always have the wisdom to know the difference.

The difference between the things I can't change and the things I can boils down to this: What am I supposed to do each day, and what can I count on the creator to do? Which part of each day is God's job, and which part is mine? I can change my part; I can't change God's part.

This is something you'll hear me say again and again: My part is to suit up; show up; and bring my common sense, intelligence, and blessings to the game of life every day—and leave the results to God.

Inner Voice
Whispers

Suit up, show up, and use your gifts. Know what part is yours and what part belongs to the universe. Do your part; the results are out of your hands.

It really is as simple as it sounds. The challenge is that although it's simple, it's not easy. It takes practice and commitment. You have to keep working at it, because it's so easy to slide back into the warrior habit of trying to control things you can't.

This lesson was brought home to me several years ago, when I was filming a television show. José, one of the first life coaches I met when I went to Hawaii, was here in Florida, and he tagged along to the studio for the shoot. It was a grueling day. A whole crew of actors, a director, and production staffers were there, and we worked for at least 12 hours, doing multiple takes of every scene. We finally wrapped up at about seven o'clock in the evening, all of us tired and hungry, and I asked to see some of the footage.

Several of us, including José, went into the edit bay to watch the clips. I was hypercritical, saying things like, "We could have done that better" and "We should shoot that scene over." All of a sudden, José clapped his hands and said, "Whoa! Whoa!"

I was taken aback. José was just there to visit and do some coaching with me. I'd invited him along on the shoot because

I thought he would find it interesting to see how we shoot an infomercial. But he didn't know anything about what was going on technically or the business the show was about. My first thought was that he was out of line to say anything at all. But that never stopped José. He got everyone's attention and said, "Time out, Russ, time out. Listen, you have prepared for this show. You came here early. You rehearsed it. You've been working on it for weeks. And you did the best job you could do. Your work here is done. The results are in God's hands now. Go on, have a nice dinner, get a good night's sleep, and I'll see you tomorrow."

What a wake-up call! All we can do is all we can do—and all we can do is enough. We can't control any more than that. We need to graciously and gratefully accept our powerlessness, and willingly surrender what we can't control.

The Original Serenity Prayer

"God, give us the grace to accept with serenity
the things that cannot be changed,
Courage to change the things which should be changed,
And the wisdom to distinguish the one from the other."

— Reinhold Niebuhr

Playing by New Rules

Living in the present without a bunch of negative emotional baggage sounds like it ought to be easy to do, but it takes practice. What made this difficult for me in the beginning was this: If I didn't have anger, anxiety, frustration, fear, doubt, guilt, and shame anymore, then who was I? If I wasn't letting ugly memories and negative emotions influence me, was I a phony? To live in the present, did I have to be something I wasn't? What would happen to the core me? I eventually learned that these are normal and natural questions, and you'll find yourself asking them as you go along. The answer is this: You will never have to pretend to be something you aren't. When you leave all those negative emotions behind, you will find your true self and your true reason for being.

Here's something else I learned that may make you very uncomfortable: Living in the present is a lot easier when we let go of our cell phones and other connected electronic devices. Cell phone addiction is a real problem today. When I got to Hawaii, one of the first things that happened was that my cell phone was taken away and locked up. I got to use it for a limited amount of time each day. At first, that caused me a great deal of anxiety. Then I realized that this restriction allowed me to focus on what was happening to me at the moment, without the distraction of constant interruptions in the form of e-mails, text messages, and calls. And there was nothing so "important" that it couldn't wait. I'm not saying don't use technology; I'm saying don't use it at the expense of yourself and your ability to live in the now. Nonstop, instant, real-time, immediate electronic communication doesn't mean you're living in the now—in fact, it could be interpreted as arrogance and a lack of respect for the people you're with at the moment.

One more critical thing to remember about living in the present is this: Where you are today isn't where you were yesterday or where you'll be tomorrow. You must keep seeking, keep learning, keep doing, keep taking action so that the plan for your life will continue to unveil itself. The Discovery Chart is the most effective and efficient tool for doing that; it's the way you'll uncover your purpose and spark your passion. In the next chapter, I'll explain how it can work for you.

CHAPTER FIVE

DISCOVERY: LOOK BACK AND MOVE FORWARD

As I was learning about the inner voice, I experienced the whole gamut of reactions: Sometimes it seemed too complicated and deep for any ordinary person to grasp (it isn't), sometimes it seemed too difficult (anyone can do it if they try), sometimes it just didn't make any sense (eventually it became clear), and sometimes it was stuff I'd heard before (but was now hearing in a context that I could understand and use). The Inner Voice way of life isn't new; it's existed since the dawn of creation. It's not a fad; once they get it, very few people ever give it up, because they don't want to go back to the old, frustrating way of living and struggling with life's challenges.

The biggest key to living the Inner Voice way of life is cleaning out all the garbage that has blocked you from having conscious contact with your inner voice. The Discovery Chart helps you do that; it helps you connect the dots backward so that you can understand why you feel and act the way you do. The Discovery Chart is the tool we use to figure out exactly the following things:

- Why we are who we are
- Why we behave the way we do (both good and bad)
- Why we have certain beliefs
- Which beliefs are real and which are imaginary
- How to maintain a state of joyfulness and peacefulness every day

- How to live without anger, anxiety, frustration, fear, doubt, guilt, or shame

- How our childhood experiences shape who we are and who we will become

- How our fears, angers, and resentments have molded us—and how to change if we're not who we were meant to be

- How to unlock our true purpose and develop an ever-growing passion to carry forward the plan for our lives

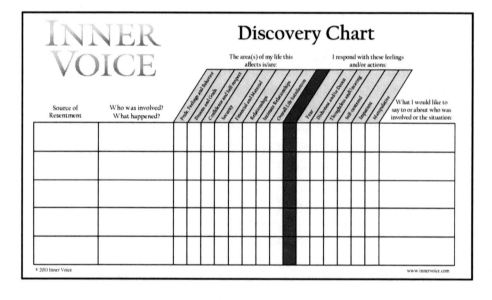

I first came across the concept of the Discovery Chart while working with a number of different spiritual leaders, and then I blended it with a program I developed many years ago called "The One-in-a-Million 90-Day Challenge." The idea is to go back into our pasts and figure out exactly why we are who we are today. Once we know that, we can make changes that will improve our lives and the lives of others as well.

When I did my first Discovery Chart, I didn't have an actual chart to use. I was told to simply write down all my fears, angers, and resentments. So I made a list of all the people I felt had harmed me either physically or emotionally during my life, along with the impact their behavior had had on me. Most of those people were from my childhood, although there were and still are some from my adult years. The process made me realize that I hadn't truly dealt with those old issues; I'd just buried them. More important, it helped me connect the dots of my life backward to understand how I got to where I was, and figure out where I needed to go. It helped me figure out my true purpose; once I did that, I developed a passion for it.

It will be easier for you to understand what I'm getting ready to explain if you look at the Discovery Chart on the previous page, and there are additional charts at the back of the book. While you can work through the Discovery Chart process alone, it's best to have a trained Inner Voice coach with you, either in person or on the phone. The coach can keep you on track and focused so that you don't get bogged down by the hurts of the past but, rather, identify them, understand how they've affected you, and figure out how to repair the damage and move forward to unlock your own purpose. Once that's done, your passion will develop and grow.

The Discovery Chart is an incredibly powerful tool—and a key reason for its power is its simplicity. All it takes is some private time, ideally with an Inner Voice coach, and a commitment to be honest with yourself and work through the questions. You can connect with an Inner Voice coach on our website at www.inner voice.com/book. In the next chapter, we'll go through the process step by step, but it will help if we first discuss some of the broader issues related to the Discovery Chart.

Two Selves, Two Sides

We all have what I call "human character assets and defects" that we have acquired along the way of our life's journey. Our character assets are our positive attributes, and our defects are our negative attributes. It's important that you understand this: Your defects don't have to be permanent; they're simply challenges you must overcome in order to live out your purpose in the way you were intended.

Inner Voice Whispers

We are the masters of our destiny. Using Inner Voice principles and strategies puts you in a position of control over your own peace of mind, body, and soul. You are also in control of your anger, fear, resentment, guilt, and shame—and ultimately your own happiness or unhappiness. It's a choice you have the power to make.

Most of us learn our defects through faulty human training, the training we receive from our parents, siblings, teachers, and other human role models. Remember that role models can be good or bad, or a combination. Most of us have all three: good, bad, and both.

If you're like the rest of us humans, it's likely that you've adopted these defects that you've learned from your various role models as the "truth" about who you are, when in fact they may be diametrically opposite of who you were meant to be. Some people think this training begins in the womb (or even before), but that's a discussion for another time. It certainly begins at birth. It's the training that directly or indirectly teaches you how to respond to your environment, what you have to do to avoid pain and achieve pleasure. Many of these lessons go back beyond our ability to remember, and they come from sources that are, when you understand them, often shocking.

From a physical perspective, there's only one of each of us. But although you may have just one body, you have two distinct people inside: your human self and your soul self.

Your human self is the person that was formed by earthly teachings, the human training. My human self was taught to respond to life in a way that my soul self would never do; my human self learned how to do things my soul self can't do. This is what human training taught me, and that's what it teaches most of us. The soul self is fundamentally incapable of being a warrior and doing negative or hurtful warrior-like things. I'm going to list some of those behaviors; as you read them, don't get distracted by thinking of which ones you do and don't exhibit.

The defects human training can breed in us usually include the following, in one form or another:

- Arrogance
- Selfish
- Self-centered
- Judgmental
- Blaming
- Critical
- Sarcastic
- Self-pitying
- Gossiping
- Pride

- Anger
- Gluttony (overdoing anything; not just food related)
- Greed
- Lust
- Envy
- Laziness
- Procrastination

This isn't a complete list. You and I could both add plenty to it; the point is to not get caught up in the minutiae, but to understand the concept. When you go through the Discovery Chart exercise, you will identify your particular character defects so that you can begin to work on correcting them.

By contrast, your soul self has none of these character defects, it doesn't operate with the same behaviors as your human self. Your soul self isn't controlling or manipulative; it's always searching for the truth and always seeking self-improvement. Your soul self operates from these character traits:

- Humility
- Honesty

- Tolerance

- Patience

- Kindness

- Trust

- Love

- Forgiveness

Because most of us are in our warrior phase during our youth and younger adult years, our human selves tend to overshadow our soul selves. Many of us find that the soul self begins to emerge around age 40, when we typically move from the warrior phase into the statesperson phase. But don't get distracted by the standard of the age of 40; the emergence of the soul self can happen at any time. The soul self may also manifest at a variety of points in our lives generated by circumstances rather than time, perhaps as a result of some sort of tragedy or major challenge, such as a near-death experience, the loss of a family member, a major illness, or some other trauma that causes us to take a serious look at our lives. It's a natural evolution.

This discussion of human self and soul self may raise this question in your mind: Does the body have a soul? That's not really the point here. The point is that our human selves are flawed and our soul selves strive to mature with the thoughts and behaviors that get us closer to the creator. One of the reasons we are here on this earth is to mature our souls, which is why we want our soul selves to be in control of our lives as much as possible. This was an interesting concept for me to learn, because I was raised according to the tenets of traditional mainstream religions and was taught that we each have a soul and that when we die, our physical bodies decay and our souls go somewhere. That "somewhere" could be heaven, which I visualized as a peaceful place far up in the sky with beautiful, fluffy clouds; gold streets; and angels—an eternal paradise. Or that "somewhere," as I was taught in my earlier years, could be hell, which I visualized as a horrible inferno. I learned these images from my childhood teachings and never stopped to consider that there might be another meaning or image that was more appropriate, or that our souls had character assets that perhaps I hadn't learned yet. As I began to understand and have conscious contact with my inner voice, I have come to the belief that the body doesn't have a soul, but rather the soul has a body. Now, that's an issue beyond the scope of this book, but I invite you to visit www.InnerVoice.com/book for discussions about that and more. What matters for our purposes is the understanding that there are essentially two people—or some might call them two energies—within each of us.

I was a slow learner, well past 40 before I had reason to get in touch with my soul self. What brought it out was a series of life crushings: the end of my 29-year marriage, unwarranted government investigations of my business, the loss of a company I had spent much of my life building, and the sense that I had failed people who depended on me. I wish I could tell you that a light went on and I had instant understanding—and that it probably will happen that way for you, too. But the reality is that's not how it happened for me and it's not how it's likely to happen for you. As I recovered from the life crushings, I went through a series of Inner Voice Awakenings, and you likely will, too. Remember, patience is a character trait of the soul self. So . . . be patient.

Inner Voice Whispers

The gift of life is in the struggle. Without the struggle, we would not build the strength and persistence to grow to our full potential.

Never Good Enough? You're in Good Company

Many of us grow up wrestling with what I call the "never-good-enough syndrome." It's a condition that can be either an extraordinarily motivating force or absolutely debilitating. If, as I did, you suffer from never-good-enough syndrome, your ultimate goal is to cure it. But that takes time, so until you do, let's talk about how to cope with it. Never-good-enough syndrome usually develops through messages we receive as children from well-meaning (and sometimes not-so-well-meaning) adults.

LIVING THE INNER VOICE LIFE

I Am Good Enough—and So Are You!

For most of my life, I felt as if no matter how much I accomplished, I could have done more or could have done it better. Using the Discovery Chart helped me realize that these feelings were the direct result of being bombarded with negative messages from my father while I was growing up. I'm sure he thought he was motivating me to improve, but the actual result was to make me feel insecure and frightened, and that was affecting my adult relationships and even my marriage.

Working through the Discovery Chart gave me the understanding I needed to recognize my character defects—the ones I really have, not the ones my father told me I had—and come up with a plan to turn those defects into character assets. Most important is that I've finally come to believe that I really am good enough, that I don't have to accept or live under the limitations and negativity of other humans. I only have to live up to the expectations set for me by God, and He will give me what I need to carry out His plan. The Inner Voice strategies helped me learn how to apply that in my life.

— Walt,
business administrator

Sometimes the adults are genuinely trying to shield the child from pain and disappointment. For example, a child who isn't a particularly good actor announces her intention to try out for the lead in the school play. Her mother cautions her that the competition is likely to be stiff and chances are slim that she'll win the role. While that may be true, the message the child hears is this: "You're not good enough." Or a teenager expresses a desire to be on the high-school football team. His father points out that he's only average height and build, and not very coordinated, so he shouldn't expect to make the cut. Again, the statement may be true, but the message received is "You're not good enough."

Sometimes the adults are trying to help the child improve. For example, instead of praising a youngster's initiative when he makes his bed, a parent points out the bunched-up sheets and does it over. Or a parent points to a high-achieving sibling and says, "Why can't you be more like that?" with the intention of helping you set a goal. The real message is "You're not good enough."

In my case, I had a stepmother who made it a point to tell me regularly that whatever I did wasn't right: I didn't do the dishes right. I didn't walk the dog right. I didn't fold my clothes right. Even had this not been coupled with other forms of abuse, her words drilled into me that I wasn't good enough. It was a horrible way to grow up. And even as a young adult, I continued to receive well-meaning advice that reinforced her message, such as the advice from people who tried to discourage me from attempting to improve my circumstances beyond my traditional job.

Some people deal with never-good-enough syndrome by allowing it to become a self-fulfilling prophecy. They live a life of mediocrity or worse. Others do what I did: They work as hard as they can to show the people who said they weren't good enough that they were wrong. I studied harder than most people do. I got up earlier and stayed up later. I figured out what my competitors were doing and did it better. Now, there's nothing wrong with working hard, but you'll never be satisfied with the results unless you're driven by the right reasons—and proving someone else wrong is rarely a right reason. If you suffer from never-good-enough syndrome, here's the best news of all: When you understand your purpose and develop your passion, when you are in conscious contact with your inner voice, you'll find that you are indeed "good enough" and that you're just as effective—and often even more so—by working half as much as you used to.

What Drives You?

When I was 20 years old, I started reading the get-rich ads in the backs of magazines. As I've explained, I was a high-school dropout, I had just been released from prison, and I'd been told over and over by too many people that I would never amount to anything. But one voice—what I now know was my inner voice—was telling me that I could do better. I heard that voice, and I was trying to figure out how. I sent away for some of the products those magazine ads promoted with such blurbs as "mail-order millions" and "make a gazillion dollars stuffing envelopes from home without ever getting out of bed," but I soon realized that those "opportunities" wouldn't work for me. Finally, I saw an ad for a $10 book on real estate investing. That book gave me the idea that I could become a millionaire, so I bought it. And by the time I finished reading it, I believed that I could, indeed, achieve that goal. I knew it meant work, so I began taking action to make it happen.

At the time, I thought I was driven by the desire to make money. What I wouldn't understand until many years later was that it was never about the money. I wasn't driven by the big

Inner Voice Whispers

When we understand why we have fears, angers, and resentments, the healing can begin.

LIVING THE INNER VOICE LIFE

Learning to Forgive

I was in a new position that required me to work closely with an employee who had been with our company for many years. She was in a trusted position and handled large sums of money. After repeatedly requesting some year-end figures from her without results, I decided that she was either extremely disorganized or possibly embezzling funds. As I continued to try to do my job and pressed for the information I needed, our relationship became strained, even rising to the level of abusive on her part. I took my concerns to some key senior people, but nothing changed. I felt abandoned, betrayed, abused, frightened, and totally resentful. The situation became intolerable, and I finally resigned.

Several months later, I received a call from the company's owner, who confirmed that my suspicions were accurate. The employee had embezzled millions of dollars, and when her theft was discovered, she had taken her own life.

I took no satisfaction in knowing that I'd been right. I had a very hard time letting go of resentment and found it almost impossible to forgive—until I was introduced to the Inner Voice way of life. I realized I was powerless over the situation and needed to surrender my resentment to a higher power (the God of my understanding). With the help of the Inner Voice program and the support of others who live the Inner Voice way of life, I was able to stop judging. Best of all, I learned to forgive not just the employee who had stolen, but also the executives who hadn't believed me when I had begun to suspect what was going on.

— Candace,
controller

houses, expensive cars, and other material trappings of wealth—although I did and still do enjoy those luxuries. But what was really driving me was the pain from my childhood. That pain gave me the burning desire to succeed, to show all those people who had told me I was nothing and no good, who told me I'd never amount to anything, that I was indeed someone. And the only way I knew to measure success at the time was with dollars. When my inner voice told me I could do better, I interpreted that to mean I could make more money than I was making in my factory job, and I believed it. Next, my inner voice spoke to me through that book, which gave me the message that anyone could become a millionaire by following the right plan. A person's level of education, background, or available money

Inner Voice Whispers

You were born with a specific genius and a gift. This is so that you can do your part to make this world a better place. All of us have a role that we're uniquely suited for.

didn't matter. From there, still unconsciously guided by my inner voice, I formulated and implemented a plan to build material wealth—and I was successful.

As I continued to feed my mind and soul with this new information, I matured—and my relationship with my inner voice did also. Looking back, I can see that while I still had unconscious contact with it, the message became clearer. As time went on, I realized I wanted to leave a legacy for my children that would make them proud of me. I wanted to help people who were less fortunate. I wanted to provide safe, decent, affordable housing for people who needed it. I wanted to build a business that would be the leader in its industry, that would provide jobs and opportunity for its employees and suppliers, and that would make a positive difference in the lives of its customers. I wanted to teach people what I knew so that they wouldn't have to learn it the hard way, as I did. All of those things are far bigger than money, and today it's very clear to me that we need a reason bigger than money if we're going to succeed.

For the most part, I understood what my drivers were, but I didn't understand why. In warrior mode, the why didn't really matter to me; I was just out there doing battle. But part of evolving into the statesperson phase includes recognizing, accepting, and dealing with the why. The Discovery Chart allowed me to do that.

Never-Ending Encores

The first time you complete your Discovery Chart is like the main part of a concert: it takes the most time, is the most challenging, and produces the most noticeable results. But, as it often happens at concerts, there are encores. The Discovery Chart isn't something you do only once. You can do a Discovery Chart anytime, for any reason. You can cover your entire life or just one isolated incident. If you've already done a Discovery Chart but find yourself tangled in a situation you can't resolve, do a Discovery Chart for that. Whatever the challenge—a work problem, relationship difficulty, or health issue—a Discovery Chart can help you solve it and get back to being happy, joyful, and free. And while it's always best to do your Discovery Charts on paper, after you've done a few, you might be able to do them in your head, if the issue is fairly focused.

This is an awesome tool. Are you ready to give it a try?

CHAPTER SIX

YOUR FIRST
DISCOVERY CHART

"If you want what I got, you gotta do what I do."

That's what one of my mentors told me early in this spiritual Inner Voice journey. I was commenting on the aura of peace, contentment, and happiness that always seemed to emanate from this man and how much I wanted to find that for myself.

When he said that, it stopped me in my tracks—even though I wasn't completely sure what it meant. But when I started thinking about it, I realized that I had been saying essentially the same thing over the years to the students who came to me for wealth-building education, although back then I was talking about making money, not spiritual development, and speaking as a warrior, not a statesperson. In virtually every speech, every class, every book, every article, I said or wrote some version of "The business and investing strategies I'm teaching you have been proven. They work, but only if you work. If you use them correctly, you'll make money. But you have to do it. You can't just sit and wish for things to happen."

I had made money, but I wanted more than that. I wanted what he had. So I studied what my mentor did and learned how to do it myself. Now, to use his vernacular, here's "what I got": I've made money. I've discovered my purpose. I've cultivated my passion for living out my life's purpose. My life is joyful, and I'm at peace most of every day. I want the same for you, and if you want the same, then the time has come to do what I and others who practice the Inner Voice way of life do.

It's time to complete your first Discovery Chart.

When I was first introduced to the idea of the Discovery Chart, I wasn't sure I wanted to look back and dredge up all those negative feelings. What I didn't realize was that the process would help me actually deal with those emotions, not just ignore them. The Discovery Chart is designed to help you understand yourself. It gives you the opportunity to confront the anger, fears, and resentments that may have kept you trapped and the chance to free yourself from them. And then it's a map that shows you where you've been and where you need to go to find your purpose and develop a passion for it.

Let's begin with some guidelines. Don't rush through this. Set aside at least an hour or so to do it the first time. My first Discovery Chart took me several uninterrupted hours, but I was doing it alone and without the structure of the Inner Voice Discovery Chart. You're getting the benefit of what I learned the hard way, so it should go much quicker for you.

Before you start, find a private place where you won't be disturbed. I recommend that, if at all possible, you work with a certified Inner Voice coach, especially as you do your first chart. The process of doing a Discovery Chart involves reaching back into the past, and you may experience some very intense emotions; don't try to repress them and don't minimize them. Respect your feelings; whatever they are, they're valid. Get them out so that you can turn them into something positive. If you are able to do this with an Inner Voice coach, let that person help as you work to understand and manage your feelings.

It's been my experience that it's best to handwrite your thoughts on paper. I feel that it keeps you more closely connected to the process. Don't worry about your penmanship, spelling, or sentence structure; this isn't a test that's going to be graded, and no one is going to see it but you and your coach. You can photocopy the charts in the back of the book, or visit www.InnerVoice.com/book and download a larger version.

Work on one issue at a time. When you first sit down and start thinking of your various resentments, angers, and fears, your mind may be flooded with memories of people, places, and things that have generated these feelings in you. If that happens, go ahead and write them all down; get them out so that you don't forget any. Once you've done that, be thoughtful, deliberate, and focused as you work through the rest of the chart for each issue.

Let's begin with an overview of the Discovery Chart process. When you've named the source of your angers, resentments, and fears, move across the chart. Write about what happened, how it affected you, how you responded, and what you'd like to say to or about the person involved. You don't need to go into minute detail; focus on the nature of the wrong and its impact on you. For example, if I were to list every single abusive thing my stepmother ever did to me (from simple beatings to burning my hand by holding it on a hot stove to forcing me to eat my own vomit when I got sick), that would be a book by itself, a book that would have no point and that no one would want to read. So on my Discovery Chart, I just wrote down her name and that she physically and emotionally abused me. Then I concentrated on addressing what her actions did to me, how they affected my adult behavior, and what I needed to do to correct any character defects I'd developed as a result.

Remember the Discovery Chart is your perception, and that's the only reality you need to be concerned with right now. The people you list may have their own perceptions of what happened. For example, I wouldn't be surprised if my stepmother's perception of the abusive things she did to me was that it was just the discipline that every child needs, or that if the perception of some of the people I have listed on my chart who betrayed me in business was that what they did was really best for the company. This isn't a trial or a test, and you don't have to prove anything. Their motives don't matter. The goal is to get to the root of why you behave the way you do.

Note that the Discovery Chart is actually three charts: one for angers, one for resentments, and one for fears. This is because it's important for you to distinguish your emotions. Some people and situations will belong clearly in a single category; others will overlap into two or all three categories. You might be able to complete your chart using just one sheet of paper for each category, or you might need multiple sheets. Whatever you need is what you need, and it's okay.

Let's walk through the chart.

Completing Your Discovery Chart

Source of Anger, Resentment, and Fear

The first column is where you list the person, institution, or situation that you feel anger or resentment toward or that you fear. For Discovery Chart purposes, fear can include feelings of guilt and shame; this is especially common when people are dealing with childhood physical and sexual abuse. Use the appropriate form for each emotion.

When I did my first Discovery Chart, I filled up this column with things that happened with my stepmother, father, and uncle; high-school incidents; the death of my father; business situations; and more. I've seen others write down things such as the following:

- Overbearing parents (resentment)
- Bullies in school (fear)
- Co-workers who get special treatment (resentment)
- Abusive teachers (anger, fear)
- Cruel classmates and neighbors (fear, resentment)
- Obnoxious bosses (anger, fear)
- Sexual predators (fear)
- Thoughtless friends or relatives (anger, resentment)

As you think about who and what to include, keep in mind that there's no such thing as "a little" anything—no such thing as a little anger, a little resentment, or a little fear. You either feel anger, resentment, or fear, or you don't. If you think of something but wonder if it's worth writing down because there was only "a little" of it, include it on your Discovery Chart. It's easy to blow off something because you've suppressed it for years, you want to forget it, or you think you may have exaggerated it. When I was in Hawaii, I underwent hypnosis to help me remember what had happened to me. I asked the hypnotherapist if I'd been exaggerating the abuse; she told me no, that it had actually been far worse than I consciously remembered.

Inner Voice Whispers

The only person you should compare yourself to is yourself. Your obligation is to do your very best. Don't worry about how that compares to someone else.

You can't forget whatever is making you angry, afraid, or resentful until you deal with it (and you might never be able to forget it, even after you deal with it). And whether you're exaggerating or not doesn't matter if what you recall is affecting you; remember, this is your perception, and reality isn't important.

For example, one of our Inner Voice members grew up in what appeared to be a model family. His parents had been married for more than 40 years, all the family members seemed to be close, and no one was openly estranged. But when this fellow was young, he had witnessed some violent outbursts and physical confrontations between his mom and dad. He's never discussed it with his parents, and they seemed to have worked out whatever caused those incidents. But as a child at the time, he felt frightened and unsafe, and those feelings were ingrained in his memory and affecting him as an adult far more than he realized. It didn't come out until we sat down and I helped him do his first Discovery Chart.

Another one of our Inner Voice members was sexually abused as a child. Although she had processed her feelings toward the family "friend" who had repeatedly molested her, she didn't realize until she began working on her Discovery Chart that she'd been harboring a great deal of anger toward her mother for failing to protect her from a predator.

When I did my first Discovery Chart, most of my angers, fears, and resentments were rooted in childhood experiences. It won't be that way for everyone, and it might not be that way for you. You may find that a larger percentage or even the majority of sources of your angers, fears, and resentments are from your adult years. For example, Jim, one of our Inner Voice members, listed a boss from early in his career. This manager never talked to Jim unless he'd done something wrong. The manager's corrections ranged from minor to major but never included any positive discussion. For years after Jim moved on to different companies and had different bosses, he felt fear and anxiety every time a manager spoke to him, especially if he was asked to come into a private meeting.

*Inner Voice
Whispers*

You are exactly where you are supposed to be right now. This is your place on the learning curve of life. If you want things to get better, you have to get better—you have to grow.

Who Was Involved? What Happened?

Once you've named the source, move to the next column on the chart and describe what happened, including the people who were involved that you didn't list in the first column. Go into as much or as little detail as is necessary for you to completely identify the actions that caused your feelings. Don't hide or mini-mize anything; you can't deal with it if you don't first recognize and admit that it happened. On the other hand, don't spend too much time wallowing in the pain and misery. As I've already men-tioned, my stepmother did some awful things to me, but I didn't list every single beating or every incident of physical abuse; I wrote down just enough to be clear in my own mind. This is essentially a highlight reel; you don't need to watch the whole movie to get the point.

It's also important that you not make excuses for anyone who has harmed you. We know, for example, that people who were abused as children often grow up to abuse their own kids or that some people do things when they're intoxicated that they'd never do sober. While those may be causes of the harmful behavior, they're not excuses. There's a part of me that understands that my stepmother must have been driven by some horrible demons to have done the things she did to me. But that doesn't excuse her actions or change the impact they had on my life. The purpose of the Discovery Chart is to understand why you behave the way you do, not why anyone else does what they do.

The Area(s) of My Life This Affected Is/Are

Think about the impact that the experiences you just wrote about have had on you, and check the appropriate box or boxes. You might mark one, some, or all. Let's discuss each of the head-ings so that you can decide what you should check.

— **Pride, feelings and behavior.** Pride is the opposite of hu-mility and the first of what's known as the seven deadly sins (pride, anger, greed, gluttony, lust, envy, sloth). Saint Augustine defined pride as "excessive love of one's own excellence." In the context of the Discovery Chart, having your pride affected could make you defensive, keep you stuck in yesterday, and make you feel as though you needed to act as if you were something you aren't.

Even if you don't think your pride was affected, if what happened has had an impact on your feelings and behavior, check this box.

— **Dreams and goals.** Your dreams and goals are your vision for the future, and they evolve as we do. Things that happen to us can clarify, change, or even destroy our dreams and the goals we set to achieve those dreams. Have your dreams and goals changed for better or worse? What do you want to be, and do you believe that you can or can't achieve that based on what has happened?

— **Confidence and self-respect.** Did what happened have an impact on your overall sense of self-worth or personal value, either positive or negative? The never-good-enough syndrome we discussed earlier falls under the confidence and self-respect umbrella.

— **Security.** Did what happened affect your ability to feel safe today, whether that safety is physical or emotional?

— **Financial and material.** Consider the impact of what happened on your attitude about money and possessions, how you manage your finances, and your economic goals.

— **Relationships.** How did what happened affect your ability to establish and maintain a variety of relationships, including those with co-workers, neighbors, friends, and family members?

— **Intimate relationships.** How did what happened affect your romantic relationships? For example, do you fear commitment, or are you excessively needy? Or are you judgmental and critical, often blaming your partner for problems and failing to see your part in the situation? Are you able to have healthy sexual relations with your partner?

— **Overall life satisfaction.** Did this situation have an impact on how satisfied you are with your life in general, either by affecting your emotions or other circumstances?

My Discovery Chart includes checks in almost every category, but especially under "pride, feelings and behavior" and "security," because I never felt safe while I was growing up and that has affected the way I have behaved as an adult. Remember, there are no right or wrong answers to this; it's just your perception of how your life today has been affected by the angers, fears, and resentments of the past.

I Respond with These Feelings and/or Actions

Look at each heading and check the columns that describe how you felt or what you did in response to what happened. Keep in mind that this doesn't mean your immediate response to the situation; for example, that you cowered in fear because of a physical attack or that you tried to get revenge for a specific wrong. This is much broader; it's how you responded to the fact that your life was affected by the situations that caused you anger, fear, or resentment. These are broad, general categories, and you should be able to identify at least one thing that describes your response; if you can't, choose what's closest.

This is often one of the hardest parts of the Discovery Chart, because it requires a degree of self-examination and admission that may be painful. But don't let that deter you, because it can also provide some huge relief. The results are worth the effort. Generally these are warrior feelings and behaviors; facing them will help you progress to statesperson. This is the section of the Discovery Chart that reveals your character defects. We'll talk about how to address and correct your defects by turning them into assets later; for now, you just need to figure out what you're dealing with. This part of the Discovery Chart changed my life forever.

— **Fearful.** Behavior generated by fear ranges from running away (from people or situations) to aggression. Whatever you do, when it's driven by fear, it's not healthy.

79

— **Dishonest and/or deceit.** This includes not being honest with yourself *or* others, and it covers issues ranging from "little white lies" to major whoppers.

— **Thoughtless and uncaring.** This includes inconveniencing others or causing hurt by what you say and do. Often inconsideration and thoughtlessness are driven by a need to feel as if you have power and are in control.

— **Self-centered.** Sometimes you'll hear this character defect referred to as "selfish" or "self-seeking"; whatever term you use, it's acting in an "all about me" way.

— **Impatient.** Refusing to accept any delay or opposition, and expressing irritation and even anger when things don't happen the way you want and when you want.

— **Manipulative.** This is when you attempt to influence the feelings and behaviors of others for your own purposes.

When I took a good, hard, honest look at myself, I had to put a lot of check marks in this section of the chart. I had the most marks under "fearful" and "self-centered," but still plenty under "dishonest" and "thoughtless." That certainly wasn't the public, warrior face of Russ Whitney—not the Russ Whitney who donated generously to charities, who spearheaded the development of the William "Bill" Austen Youth Center in Cape Coral, who was quick to write a check to friends in need, who gave his family every material thing they wanted—and certainly not the Russ Whitney who wasn't afraid of anything or anybody. I was selfish not with money but with my time. I wasn't always honest in my relationships. And one of the ways I dealt with my insecurity was to be inconsiderate of others, because I had the power to do it—after all, I was in charge. Something else I used to do was practice sarcasm. I prided myself on my great wit and how fast I could think on my feet. I thought I was cute and funny. I now know that I was almost always more hurtful than amusing, especially when I used sarcasm with people who worked for me. I had power and authority over them, and although I didn't consciously realize it, I wanted to make sure they knew it. Doing the Discovery Chart helped me understand that I thought that if they were afraid to challenge me, the scared child inside me would remain protected and secret.

I also came to the understanding that these character defects and how I manifested them were key ingredients in my eventual humbling and the creator's way to drive me to mature my soul by learning and practicing the Inner Voice way of life.

What Would I Like to Say to or about Who Was Involved or the Situation

This is where the healing begins. This is where you get to vent, to have the last word, to say all those things you may have thought but couldn't voice at the time. Tell those people they were wrong. Cuss them out if you want to. In my original Discovery Chart, I used some language directed toward my stepmother and a few other people that I wouldn't repeat in this book. Feel free to do the same. This is your opportunity for closure.

Let me clarify that you're not going to actually say these things to anyone. Remember, we can't change the past, so there's no point in actually going back to an individual you've named, and it's possible that many of the people involved are no longer alive and you can't actually talk to them anyway. None of that matters now. Just write down what you feel. And if it helps, say it out loud, too. Do a

Inner Voice Whispers

What ultimately holds you back is your choice to be held back by one factor or another. What will always move you forward is your choice to do so, no matter what the obstacles, real or perceived, may be.

little yelling if you want; I did. It might seem a little silly, but for me, it was a chance to vent—and it worked.

But here's the important thing: You do that once, and then you're done with it. You're ready to move on. You don't keep cussing and complaining and blaming. Get it out and get it over with. This is where we start to let go of resentments and heal ourselves through the process of forgiveness.

LIVING THE INNER VOICE LIFE

Changing What We Can

I have always been a type A personality—needing to be in control, wanting to change others—because I believed I knew best, even thinking I could manipulate God or His plans. I was in a toxic relationship that I thought I could fix, and it was having a negative impact on every part of my life.

The Inner Voice program helped me understand that the only person I can change is me. More important is that when I surrender control of my life to God, I'm happier and healthier in every way. Business is great, my relationship with my son is improving, and my new romance is showing great promise. Even better is that others are encouraged by the changes they're seeing in me.

— Karl,
business owner

When Your Chart Is Complete

You'll likely feel exhilarated when you've completed your Discovery Chart. And you should, because it's a tremendous accomplishment. But don't stop there; you have plenty more to do.

Go back over your grid and start connecting the dots backward. Use one of the two approaches we discussed previously: either start from your childhood, as I did, and look at how things worked together as you grew up and progressed through adulthood, or start from today and look back. Examine your conduct or feelings, move back to the areas of your life they're related to, and move farther back to the cause. Here's how that worked for me: I was dishonest, and it was affecting my relationships. As I connected the dots backward, I saw that if my stepmother hadn't had a legitimate provocation for abusing me, she'd make one up. I didn't understand that then; I just knew that she would ask me a question and if she didn't like the answer, she'd get violent and abusive. So I tried to figure out what she wanted to hear, to anticipate what I could say that wouldn't set her off, whether it was true or not. Sometimes it worked, but it also meant that I sometimes had to lie. Doing my Discovery Chart showed me that I was sometimes dishonest in my adult relationships because I'd learned that behavior trying to protect myself from a woman I was afraid of when I was a child. When that dawned on me, I remember thinking, *I'm dishonest because of what that horrible person did to me. And the last thing I want to be is dishonest. The last thing I want to do to someone else is what she did to me.* I realized I could change that behavior, that I could turn that character defect of dishonesty into a character asset of honesty.

This was a very powerful moment for me; when I realized I was doing to others what had been done to me, I wanted to change. I wanted to turn those negative behaviors into positive ones. It was going to take some work—but first, I had to figure out how to do it.

The first step in changing is to forgive the source of your anger, resentment, and fear; usually it's a person, but it could be a group of people or another entity. You don't have to forgive the deed; you need to forgive the person. You don't necessarily have to forget what happened, and you certainly don't have to put yourself in a position for it to happen again. For example, if someone cheated you by borrowing money and not repaying it, you don't have to lend that person money the next time she asks. If someone abused you, you don't have to put yourself in a position that makes it possible for him to do it again. Forgiving doesn't make what that person did right; it just means that you get the benefit of letting it go.

When I forgive someone, I do it for me, not for the other person, even though that person may get some benefit. When I don't forgive, when I hold on to that anger and resentment, I'm sitting at home miserable while the other person is out dancing, figuratively speaking. Others don't know what I'm feeling, and if they did, they probably wouldn't care. My feelings are my responsibility. So not forgiving someone who has wronged you is as if you drink poison hoping the other person will die. When you understand that you're doing it for yourself, forgiving gets easier.

There will also be times when the injury that's the source of your anger, resentment, or fear is so deep that the feelings return even after you've gone through the steps of dealing with them. For example, it took me a while, but I've forgiven my stepmother for all the horrible things she did to me. I've identified the areas of my life that her actions affected and the character defects that resulted. I still have to work on those defects, but I'm no longer angry or afraid.

By contrast, I'm still struggling with a business situation that occurred years ago. Here's that story: It wasn't unusual for my financial training company to partner with other educational product companies so that we could reach more people. Some of those partnerships were successful, others not so much; that's all part of the ebb and flow of business. But there's one deal that I did years ago that I still feel resentment about, and I still have to work on those feelings. At the time, my company was doing extraordinarily well: growing, profitable, with plenty of cash. This other company, a private company owned by a few people, was on the verge of bankruptcy, but it had a customer base that we weren't reaching. The owners and I reached an agreement to develop a training package under the other company's brand that turned out to be very successful and profitable, and it's still operating today. Most of the time, I'm okay with that, but sometimes, I still resent that I was forced out of my company and that the owners of the other company are still benefiting from what I did for them while I was running my company. I know it's not a rational resentment; those people had nothing to do with what happened to me, and it shouldn't matter that their fortunes soared due largely to my efforts, even as I was struggling. But sometimes it does. And when I start feeling that resentment, I have to make a conscious effort to stop and work on those feelings by surrendering them. I get in a quiet place and turn it over to God, who has told me—more than once!—that what I did for the owners of the other company, I did for Him and that I would have success going forward, although my new success would be equal or better, but not the same.

Forgiveness is a process, not an event—especially when the wrong is major. It would be nice if we could forgive instantly and never have to deal with whatever happened again, but that's not how it happens. We choose to forgive, and sometimes we have to make that choice over and over. Here's something interesting: The Aramaic word for *forgive* means "to untie." When you forgive, you untie yourself from the hurt, pain, anger, and burden you carry from that, and you free yourself to live a successful and happy life.

Inner Voice Whispers

Holding on to past hurts is like holding on to a giant rock. You feel more pain and burden than the other person will ever know. However justified you may be, however enormous the hurt, forgive and release the burden for yourself.

We can intellectually understand the benefits of forgiving and still have a hard time doing it. Beyond surrendering, there are a few other things you can do that will help you forgive those who've harmed you. One is to acknowledge and feel the pain they've caused. Don't downplay it, and certainly don't try to pretend it didn't happen. It can be helpful to share your feelings, but it must be with the right person, someone who knows how to help you process your feelings and heal, rather than encourage, your bitterness. If you're not sure whom to talk with, contact an Inner Voice coach for guidance. You can find information about Inner Voice coaches online at www.innervoice.com/book.

It can also be helpful to keep a journal. Sometimes just writing down our feelings lets us release them, and it may even give us deeper insight into ourselves. If whatever you need to forgive is related to a life change, make plans for your future. For example, if your spouse wants a divorce and you don't, or if you've lost your job because of something someone else did, you need a plan for what to do next. Focusing on that may make forgiving easier. Most important, don't judge. Let judgment come from a higher power; it's not your job.

After forgiving, the next step in changing the impact of what has happened to you is to reverse the behavior, to do the opposite of the character defect you identified on your Discovery Chart. So if you're dishonest, you must begin practicing honesty. If you've been selfish, you must start putting others first. If you've been inconsiderate, you must start being considerate. This takes conscious thought and practice. It may feel uncomfortable at first. And you'll likely get some interesting reactions from the people you deal with. All of that's okay; just take it one issue at a time. Are you in a situation where you're tempted to be dishonest? Stop, think, and be honest. Did you do something selfish or inconsiderate? Apologize and make it right. Do one thing at a time.

I wish you could do a Discovery Chart once and immediately turn into a perfect spiritual being. That's not the way it happens. Things will happen after you've done your first chart that you're going to need to deal with using the structure of the Discovery Chart. Eventually this process will become so ingrained that you'll do it instinctively; you won't need to write it down. But until you are absolutely certain you have achieved that level of spiritual growth, use the paper chart.

We can't change the past. We can't rewind and do things over. This is simply out of our control. What we can control is how we feel and what we do today, but to do that requires an understanding of who we are and why we act as we do.

Your Purpose Revealed

I believe our creator (the God of our understanding) has a purpose for us, and that purpose is revealed through our struggles. As you study your Discovery Chart, connect the dots backward, and put together your plan for changing your character defects into assets, you'll begin to see your purpose. And when you do, you'll develop a passion for it that will give you the greatest odds for success.

But you won't do this alone. You'll do it with regular conscious contact with your inner voice. In the next chapter, you're going to learn how to do that.

CHAPTER SEVEN

Making Conscious Contact with the Inner Voice

Now that you know how to use the Discovery Chart to understand why you behave the way you do, identify your character defects, and start the process of determining the purpose of your life, it's time to learn how to use the inner voice to develop a plan to change those defects into assets and live out your purpose.

The term *inner voice* has two key definitions:

1. It's the means by which you communicate with the God of your understanding: the universe, the creator, your higher power; choose the term you use now or the one you want to use in the future. It's not the name that counts; it's the conscious contact and personal relationship that you want to develop.

2. It's a daily and lifelong program that helps you figure out where you are, where you want to be, and how you're going to get there.

In later chapters, we'll talk more about the Inner Voice as a program that gives you the structure and support you need to get on track, stay on track, and recognize when you're off track. First you need to learn how to harness the strength and power of clear, purposeful communication with the inner voice.

We all have contact with the inner voice. Sometimes it's conscious; sometimes it's unconscious. The unconscious contact is certainly better than nothing, but the conscious contact is where we find the definite direction that allows us to minimize the possibility of mistakes and failures as we maximize our individual potential.

Remember, when I did my first Discovery Chart and connected the dots backward, I realized that it had been unconscious contact with my inner voice that had pushed me to get a book on how to invest in real estate when I was just 20 years old. I didn't know anything about real estate. As I've told you, I was looking at opportunity ads in the back of a magazine when I saw the ad for that book that promised to teach me how to make money. I had no idea what it was about or what I was getting into; I just felt compelled to make the purchase. The book itself was $10; at the time, I was only making about $6 an hour, with a wife to support and a baby on the way. So the expense was fairly significant, but something told me it would be worth it.

In addition to actual investing strategies, the book told me things I'd never heard from anyone else before. It told me I could get into business with little money and virtually no credit. It told me that it didn't matter that I was a high-school dropout, my parents were alcoholics, I'd been abused, or I'd gotten involved with the wrong crowd and ended up in prison—I could still have the life I dreamed of and more. It told me I could become a millionaire. Even though I didn't understand it at the time, today I know that this message was definitely from unconscious contact with my inner voice. And if this story is making you think of a time when something similar happened to you, make a note of it and use that information as you connect the dots backward to identify your purpose.

The day the book came in the mail, I started reading it after dinner and got so excited I couldn't stand it. I stayed up all night to finish it—and several times even woke up my wife to share parts of it with her. It makes me smile now to remember that as much as she supported me, she would have been just as happy if I'd waited until morning to tell her what I was learning. By the time the sun came up, that same unconscious contact with my inner voice had begun telling me that I was going to become a millionaire by investing in real estate. I didn't completely understand it and I had no idea how it was all going to work, but I believed it and I was ready to get started.

Of course, everybody I knew tried to talk me out of it. They tried to tell me that what I had was a good-enough life and that I shouldn't expect more. They pointed out all the problems I might encounter in real estate, such as if the tenants moved out, if the roof leaked, and if the plumbing backed up. They reminded me that I had no experience with real estate or investing. And they attacked the author of the book, telling me that I shouldn't believe anything those "get-rich" books said.

Inner Voice Whispers

Be quiet in the morning and think about the day. Let a few key things come to mind. Don't "work" on your to-do list; don't force it. Let life flow and watch your productivity grow.

But that inner voice kept telling me I could do it; and maybe more important, if you recall, I didn't know that I couldn't do it. My response to the naysayers was that people had been buying income properties for hundreds of years. Tenants had been renting properties for hundreds of years. Real estate investors had been getting wealthy (and wealthier) for hundreds of years. Were all the tenants going to move out just because Russ Whitney decided to buy an investment property? Of course not. And landlords have been maintaining their properties since ancient times, so if the roof leaked or the plumbing backed up, I'd just take care of it. How hard could that be? The book explained how to plan for and deal with such contingencies. Even at the age of 20, with my limited

When Your Inner Voice Says Stop, Stop!

My former husband and I are co-owners of a house in another state that we've been trying to sell for some time. The listing contract was expiring, and the real estate agent told us that the property wasn't likely to sell unless we dropped the asking price substantially. I was in favor of a price reduction; my ex wasn't.

I found myself firmly in warrior mode, trying to battle my way to a resolution without caring how many proverbial dead bodies I left in my wake. I finally calmed myself enough to use the two-way conscious contact technique of consulting my inner voice. I was clearly told to stop and surrender the situation to my creator.

My response was, "I don't think so." I had set a deadline for getting the asking price of the house lowered, and I'd decided that if my former husband didn't agree by my arbitrary date, I was going to force a sale—something that wouldn't be good for either of us. But my inner voice persisted, telling me again to surrender. And finally I listened and surrendered. Two days later, the real estate agent came up with a deal that worked for both my ex and me. The price would be lowered—not as far as I wanted, but to a level acceptable to him—for 60 days. If there was no activity after that time, we'd reduce the price to where I thought it should be. The listing contract was renewed, and we quickly received an offer that was higher than the amount I wanted. More important is that I learned to listen to my inner voice when it tells me to stop fighting.

— Barbara,
executive assistant

experience, I had enough common sense to know that the dire warnings of the naysayers were absurd.

But was it really common sense—or my inner voice? Or maybe, as I believe today, it was unconscious contact with my inner voice that gave me the common sense to realize that real estate was the vehicle I needed at the time to achieve my goals and move toward continuing to gain the life experiences that would lead me to fulfilling my purpose. It was God's plan for that part of my life.

Learning to Pay Attention

The miracle of the inner voice has been inside you and me our entire lives; you just may not have met it yet. That's where I operated for 30 years. As I've shared, in hindsight, I can see where the inner voice was directing me, but because I didn't have conscious contact with it, I either ignored it or took credit for it—even though I didn't understand that's what I was doing. Today, I realize that every time I ignored my inner voice and didn't follow its guidance, whatever I was pursuing was either very short-lived or an outright failure. Ignoring my inner voice by not doing something it was telling me to do has also cost me dearly in missed opportunities. But when I listened, things always fell into place and worked not only for my benefit but for the greater good as well.

It's important to learn to distinguish your true inner voice from what your human training is telling you. As we've discussed, human training is what we learn from human sources, from ourselves and others when we aren't in contact with the inner voice. Character defects are manifestations of human training. Now, this isn't to say that everything you learn from people is bad; that's not the case at all. In the last five years, I've learned an amazing amount from the people who've been willing to teach me—and even from some who didn't realize they were teaching me. But it's been my experience that the things that you've learned that cause you to behave in a nonspiritual way are almost always the result of human training. The things that you've learned that prevent you from reaching your full potential are from human training. The things that you've learned that drive you to do things that could hurt others are from human training.

We have the ability to rise above our human training, even when we don't realize that's what we're doing. The inner voice is usually quick to speak, quick to tell you what to do. In just about any situation, the first pure thought that comes to your mind is from your inner voice, and anything after that is from human training.

For example, let's say you're walking down a crowded hallway and you bump into someone. Your first thought is to apologize. That's a pure thought; it's your inner voice guiding you. But what often happens is that your next thought is something like, *Well, he could have said he was sorry; after all, he should have been looking where he was going* or *I don't have time to apologize right now; I'll catch her next time.* That's your human training. When it gets in the way, it can block access to your inner voice so that the pure direction you need gets lost.

Here's another example from my own experience: While I was working on this book, I was on my way home one day in moderately heavy traffic. As I approached an intersection and was slowing down for a red light, I noticed a car waiting to turn onto the street from a parking lot. In my warrior days, I probably wouldn't have noticed the car; and if I had, I would have given my time more value than the time of the person in the other car, and I would have just kept driving. But on this day, I saw that car and stopped earlier than necessary to allow room for it to turn in front of me. I probably would have completely forgotten about the incident, but a few hours later, I got a call from a woman who used to work for me. She'd moved out of state, and I didn't know she was back until she called to tell me that she was the driver of that car, that she had recognized me, and that she really appreciated my courtesy.

Your inner voice is always there, guiding you through every minute of your day. However, you may not always be able to hear it. Sometimes it gets drowned out by messages from your human training. Sometimes it will go silent because it's waiting for you to pay attention. For the most part, when my inner voice goes silent, it's because it's buried under a whole host of character defects and faulty thinking that I've learned from other humans over the years. I've learned that my inner voice goes silent when I fall into self-pity or take on the role of victim. When I engage in negative conduct, such as acting out in anger, frustration, blaming, sarcasm, and vengeance, my inner voice goes silent. But when I realize what I'm doing, when I return to what I call the Inner Voice way of life, it starts talking to me and giving me honest, unselfish, pure, loving answers again.

Inner Voice Whispers

If you plant a seed, water it for a few days, and then stop, it won't sprout and you might as well never have planted it. So keep watering your seeds. Direct your focus again and again toward those things you're committed to completing.

Two-Way Conscious Contact Changed My Life—and It Will Change Yours

How do you put the power of your own inner voice to work for you? By developing your ability to hear it through conscious contact. By learning to distinguish the difference between direction based on human training and guidance from your inner voice. The easiest way to learn how to do this is with a technique I call "two-way conscious contact." In its simplest form, two-way conscious contact is a "things-to-do list" on steroids. But once you learn to do it, see the evidence, and trust it, you'll find that it's so much more than that.

I'm going to use the terms *prayer* and *God* as I explain how to do this, but don't get hung up on semantics. The point is to communicate with your higher power, and you can call it whatever you want.

So-called time-management experts tell us to start each day by making a to-do list. I have a couple of issues with that. First, you can't manage time; time simply is. A minute is a minute; an hour is an hour. You can't do anything about that. What you can manage is yourself; you can't manage time.

Second, and more important, is that creating a to-do list on our own, without contact with the inner voice, blocks us from knowing what God wants us to do. We stay in warrior mode; we come up with a list of human tasks: things we need to do for business, household chores, and social or community work. When we use two-way conscious contact, we open that process up to a much larger universe.

Inner Voice Whispers

Test each answer you receive against the four absolutes by asking these questions:
Is it honest?
Is it pure?
Is it unselfish?
Is it loving?

This is how I learned to do two-way conscious contact, and it's how I still do it. I've found that the best time is first thing in the morning before the rest of the world starts intruding, before I check my e-mail, before anybody else in the house is awake, before any other distractions occur. I go to a quiet, comfortable place where I won't be disturbed, and I clear my mind of human thoughts. I don't think about what might be on my agenda, about the meetings I have scheduled, about the work I need to do, about what others might be expecting of me.

Ever since I began my search for the true meaning of life, I have kept a handwritten journal. I have volumes of them! I get out my journal and write, "God, creator of the universe, direct me in my thinking. Show me Your will for me today and give me the power to carry it out."

Then I sit back, close my eyes, wait for thoughts to come to my mind, and write them down. I don't analyze or judge or critique; I just write what thoughts come to me and only those thoughts. By that I mean that if a thought is about my needing to do something, that's what I write down. If it's just a name or a place, I write that down. I don't let myself get distracted at that point by thinking about how I'm going to get a particular task done, why I'm being given a name, or any other details. Remember that thoughts will come and go quickly, which is why it's important to have a journal in front of you when you do this. When the thoughts stop coming, I express my gratitude and use what my inner voice has told me as I get on with my day. I open my eyes, look at my list, and I know what I need to do that day.

It really is that simple. Don't be tempted to take this incredibly powerful tool and make it complicated; that would be your human training taking over.

It's been my experience that two-way conscious contact is most effective when practiced daily. Do it every morning, and the creator will tell you everything you need to know for that day. Remember, we're made to live in the present—not in yesterday, not in tomorrow. You won't get a solution to every problem or a plan for every idea. You will get exactly what you need for today and only today. Often what you get for today is designed to prepare you for tomorrow. As I've already said, having plans and goals for the future are great, as long as you recognize the difference between planning for the future (which creates feelings of peace and security) and trying to live there (which causes anxiety and fear).

I've developed these guidelines for practicing two-way conscious contact from my own experience and from what I've been taught by my coaches and teachers:

The Art of Listening

My business was struggling financially, and I didn't know what to do. My vision was clouded by fear and stress. But I was an entrepreneur. I was supposed to be in control—and I had a winning track record to prove it. Yet, for the first time in my life, I was dreading getting up in the morning because I had no idea what difficulties I was going to face or how I was going to manage them. I was off track, and I didn't know how to get back on.

Then I learned how to do two-way conscious contact with my inner voice. I got up in the morning, wrote down what I was grateful for and what I needed help with, and waited for the answers. And they came. Day after day, they came. Every day, I knew what to do for that day, and I didn't worry about tomorrow. I was able to get my company—but, more important, myself—back on track.

You've heard the phrase "the weight of the world was on my shoulders"; well, that's how I felt, and that weight was lifted when I learned to stay in the moment, surrender what I couldn't control, and receive and trust daily direction from my inner voice.

— Damian,
CEO

1. Do your two-way conscious contact first thing in the morning, before you do anything else, even if you have to get up a half-hour earlier than you do now. Find a place where you can relax, be comfortable, and be undisturbed. Make it clear to the other members of your household that you need them to respect your need for privacy and solitude during this time.

2. Use a journal and write down your initial prayer and all the answers you receive. I've found that writing by hand, as opposed to using a computer or recording device, keeps you in closer contact with the inner voice and the messages it's sending. It's just as important to write your prayer as it is to write the answers. Also, you're going to want to refer back to your notes, so write them in a permanent place, like a journal, that you will keep.

3. After you write your initial prayer, sit back and let your mind go blank. As thoughts start to come, write them down—all of them. Write the good thoughts, bad thoughts, reasonable thoughts, logical thoughts, crazy thoughts, and holy or unholy thoughts. Capture them immediately without judging.

4. When the flow of thoughts slows down, stop. That means you've received all you need for the day. Don't force it.

5. Test the answers to confirm if they're coming from God or your own human will. The test is simple. Just ask yourself if the thing on your list has the following characteristics:

- Honest
- Pure
- Unselfish
- Loving

In the Inner Voice community, these are known as the *four absolutes*. If the answer you receive is all four of those things, you're getting divine guidance that's safe to follow. If anything about the thought is dishonest, impure, selfish, unloving, or hateful, then it's not from the creator of the universe.

6. Obey! You have to do what you're told. I admit that this is an area that has challenged me—and still does occasionally. But I've learned that when I don't obey my inner voice messages, a crisis often shows up. When I go back through my journal and see what I have and haven't obeyed, I can see clear patterns of

evidence concerning why I should have done what I wrote down during my two-way conscious contact.

As you progress with your two-way conscious contact, you may want to be more specific in your requests, and you may also want to include things you're thankful for. For example, there were many days while I was writing this book that I began my two-way conscious contact this way: "God, thank you for the beautiful luxuries You've blessed me with: my health, my family, good friends, financial independence, and a beautiful waterfront home in southwest Florida. Guide my writing today. Direct my thoughts and words so that I'm sharing Your message, not mine, and let that message touch the hearts of those who are living in fear and doubt. God, I'm ready to have You remove all of my own character defects so that I might be of better use to You in helping others find their own paths to happiness, peace, passion, purpose, and freedom." If you're working on a major project or if something is on your mind, it's okay to address it directly with your inner voice during your daily two-way conscious contact.

Inner Voice Whispers

The odds don't determine your results, whether it's with your health, your wealth, your relationships, or anything else. What create the results you get are your thoughts, actions, words, focus, commitment, and persistence.

Don't Turn Off Your Receiver

Although you should begin your day by inviting direction from your inner voice, that morning session won't be the only time that it speaks to you. Be receptive to those messages throughout the day. You've probably been getting them all of your life; you just have a better understanding of what they are now. And always put the direction you get through the test of the four absolutes (is it honest, unselfish, pure, and loving?) to be sure it's coming from God and not your human self.

My first two-way conscious contact happened while I was in Hawaii. It wasn't anything like the process I eventually learned and have just explained to you. It was much less evolved, but it still worked. As you practice two-way conscious contact, your process will get better and more precise—and the answers you receive will, too. You'll get ongoing evidence that the answers work, which will help you trust the process more so that you are able to live without fear and doubt.

This is the story I mentioned in Chapter 2, when I told you about the concept of having God on the inside and how I tried to get God inside me by pointing to my mouth, eyes, ears, and nose while praying. That didn't work, but God clearly heard my prayer and answered it the following day. Here's what happened:

Part of the program at the retreat in Hawaii involved family counseling. My daughter had flown out for a visit, and she and I met with one of the therapists. At that time, my daughter thought I was just being a baby and a quitter. She saw me in a state that was totally opposite from the in-charge warrior father she'd known all her life, and it bewildered and angered her. Just a few minutes into our first therapy session, she said some things that were hurtful. In retrospect, she was saying things I needed to hear, and I'm grateful for her courage and willingness to come to Hawaii to be with me. However, rather than letting sharp words escalate, the therapist stopped the session and sent us for a walk on the beach; we were to just walk together, without talking, for about 15 minutes.

It was a gorgeous day. As we walked in silence, I noticed an empty beer bottle thrown up on a crest of sand. As we walked past it, the thought that came to my mind was *What a jerk, to throw trash on this beautiful beach and leave it there.* Then I felt something almost indescribable, an energy of some sort. I stopped walking.

Something was happening in my heart and my head. Something was changing inside me.

I didn't hear spoken words, but I got the message: "Pick up the bottle, son." Now, Russ Whitney in warrior mode wouldn't have left his daughter's side at that moment for anything; after all, Russ, the warrior, was focused on repairing our relationship. That was my goal, and nothing else mattered. But I felt compelled to leave her and walk about 10 yards back up the beach to get the bottle. She gave me an odd look, but as we'd been instructed by the therapist, she didn't speak.

As we walked back to the mansion, I remembered seeing some trash in the bushes on the grounds when I'd been outside the day before. At the time, I had thought that someone ought to find it and pick it up, but I had left it there. After all, picking up trash wasn't my job—or was it? With the dirty beer bottle in one hand, I detoured to those bushes, found the trash, picked it up, and found a garbage can to dispose of it.

Later that day, I was in my suite and reached for my reading glasses. One of the arms snagged on something and broke off, falling to the floor. I probably cursed and was about to kick the broken piece under a bookcase. After all, I was far too important and my time too valuable to spend it picking up the broken part of my reading glasses. Someone else could do it.

Then that same indescribable energy I'd felt earlier in the day on the beach hit me again. And it stopped me midkick. A clear thought came into my mind: *Slow down, relax, pick up the broken part of your glasses, and throw it away properly. That's just the right thing to do.* And that's what I did.

Now, you probably don't see anything special or miraculous in these simple acts of picking up someone else's trash and my broken glasses. But that's part of the point. Your conscious contact with your inner voice is something that only you will see or understand. And while picking up litter may not be a big deal for a lot of people, it was for me on that day, under those circumstances.

Later I had the opportunity to share this story with one of my spiritual counselors, and I asked if this is what it meant to have

God on the inside. He said yes and gave me some other examples of recognizing how and when we have God inside. It's not about picking up trash or being superficially pleasant; it's about learning the daily steps to find your own answers in your daily search for the truth about your own life.

Things Aren't Always What They Seem

Some of the answers you receive during your two-way conscious contact may not make sense at first, or you may misinterpret them. That's okay. Do your best, and your inner voice will provide the clarification you need.

When a random name comes through as part of your two-way conscious contact, without any clarification, just give the person a call and check in. If the person is an Inner Voice member—that is, someone who follows the Inner Voice way of life and participates in our on- and offline communities—you can simply say, "You were in my two-way conscious contact." The person will know what you mean, and together you can figure out what you're supposed to do. If the person isn't an Inner Voice member, all you need to say is, "You were on my mind, and I wanted to touch base with you and see how you're doing." Then relax and let the conversation flow naturally.

Inner Voice Whispers

If you want it *real bad*, you're going to get it *real bad*. Relax. Let it go. Surrender it, and you'll get what you're supposed to have the way you're supposed to have it.

As I've shared, my life's purpose is to help people, and my passion is teaching and sharing. So when a name comes to me during my two-way conscious contact, I've occasionally let my character defect of arrogance pop up by assuming that the person needs my help. Russ to the rescue! That's not always the case, such as when my inner voice gave me the name of a friend of mine—only his name, nothing else. So I thought, *Bob must need my help!* I called him, and we talked. He didn't seem distressed about anything. Then during the conversation, I mentioned that I was getting ready to change my computer from a PC to a Mac and was planning to get an iPad. But I was more than a little out of my depth with this purchase. I told Bob that I was going to the Apple store to get some help. He told me that he'd been using Macs for years and knew exactly what I needed. He suggested meeting me at the Apple store, about a 45-minute drive for him, to help me decide what to get. I'm well aware that he's a busy man with a wide range of business responsibilities, so this was an incredibly generous offer. That's when I realized that God had given me Bob's name, not because I was supposed to do something for him, but because I needed help and Bob was the person to provide it.

Inner Voice Whispers

Has something been gnawing at you, and your inner voice won't give you a rest from it? Get over your reluctance, get past your resistance, and get to work on getting it done. Ramp up your determination, make the commitment, and take action on it today!

Sometimes the reason the inner voice gives us a name without any instruction is because it's part of the preparation for what we need to do or learn. Make a note of the name and wait; clarification will come.

Here's a story of how that worked for me: About 35 years ago, I was involved in a car accident with someone who was seriously injured. Recently his name came up in my two-way conscious contact—just his name, nothing else. I didn't know what to do, so I did nothing. A few days later, his name came up again, this time with the message that I should contact him. I tried to find him; I searched Google, Facebook, and LinkedIn with no luck. I called the attorney who was involved in the litigation relating to the crash; he remembered the case and tried unsuccessfully to locate the family. I didn't know what else to do.

This sort of thing will happen in your two-way conscious contact. Remember that what you need will come to you at the right time—and now may not be your time. Respond to the messages you get as best you can, and let your creator handle it from there.

So, after doing all I could do to find this man without success, I surrendered the issue. The next message I got was to write this man a letter, apologize for my part in what happened, ask for forgiveness, and offer whatever help I could. Of course, I couldn't find him, so I couldn't actually send the letter, but I obeyed and wrote the letter in my journal—two heartfelt pages.

At the same time I was receiving and obeying these messages from my inner voice, I was also dealing with feelings of resentment toward a longtime employee who'd embezzled a significant amount of money and then committed suicide. It wasn't so much that I was angry as I was hurt by the betrayal. I was also hurt that this person felt she had no alternative but to take her own life. If she'd just come to me, we could have worked something out. My feelings of resentment fluctuated from nagging to overwhelming. One day, when the resentment was particularly strong, I began my two-way conscious contact with a request for help with this particular issue. Very clearly, God told me this: "If the man who suffered life-changing injuries in the car accident can forgive you, you can forgive this person."

That was so powerful that it made me break down in tears. God went back 35 years to something I'd never forgiven myself for and used it to help me learn that I can forgive anything. Forgiving is a lifesaver—not for the person being forgiven, but for the person doing the forgiving.

Wow. Think about that.

Now, has the man who was injured in the car accident forgiven me? I don't know. I don't even know if he's still alive; that's not the point. In the letter I wrote but couldn't send, I asked him to forgive me. I did that because my inner voice told me to, and we aren't told to do anything that isn't possible. I hope, for his own sake, that that man has forgiven me, because I know how damaging it is to oneself to hold on to anger and resentment. But I also know that I have no control over whether this person has forgiven me or not. However, I can control what I do, and I can forgive.

The Earth Won't Move Every Day

Many of the inner voice stories I've shared so far are significant, even earth shaking, certainly life-changing events. But two-way conscious contact is a tool that will help you with all aspects of your life, from the mundane to the monumental. Let me give you some examples from people who are living the Inner Voice way of life and practicing two-way conscious contact every day.

Denise has a somewhat-strained relationship with her father. It's not terrible, but it's not great. "In my two-way conscious contact, God told me to call my dad. I didn't do it," she told me. "A few days later, I got the message again. I still didn't call. Then God said this: 'Call your father. This is the third time I've reminded you. You can't complain about him not reaching out to you if you aren't reaching out to him.' So I called. It was a nice conversation, no big deal—except that my dad thanked me for calling. And it made me feel good."

Isaac stays in regular contact with his sisters, so he was surprised when he received the message "Call your sister" during his two-way conscious contact. He called his older sister, and she was fine. He had barely ended that call, when his younger sister called him. She was having a relationship crisis and need her big brother's shoulder to cry on. This shows us how the universe steps in with a bit of correction when we need it.

Here's another example of how your inner voice will nag you to do what you're told: Warren got the message "Walk the dog" during his two-way conscious contact. He was busy and under a lot of pressure, and taking care of the dog was the kids' responsibility. He ignored the message—until he got it again. So he took the dog out for a long walk. "I got away from the house, the kids, all the things I was worrying about. I was reminded of all the beauty in the world, and I felt a wonderful sense of peace," he said. The dog got some needed exercise, but the real beneficiary of the walk was Warren.

Finally, there's Blake, who has smoked cigarettes for probably close to 40 years. One morning, during the answer part of his two-way conscious contact, he wrote, "Take it easy and allow me to cleanse your body of the damage you've done by smoking. I will help you, but you need the desire to stop." He had tried and failed to quit smoking countless times in the past, and he wasn't sure what to do with that message. A week later, his doctor told him he needed to quit and suggested a new smoking-cessation program. As I write this, he hasn't completely quit yet, but he is smoking less than half the amount he used to and is making progress every day.

Inner Voice Whispers

Even though I might think that I need to fix everything and everybody, the reality is that I need more fixing myself than I can ever possibly do for others.

Even though your two-way conscious contact won't always be momentous, it's always important. And it's important that you have conscious contact with your inner voice every day, whether you do it using the two-way method you've just learned or some other way. It takes discipline, but it's what keeps you progressing to statesperson and beyond. I admit that there have been times when I was lazy about doing conscious contact, and I've paid the price by getting out of balance. Fortunately, we're built with alarm bells to remind us when we're either doing something we shouldn't or not doing something we should. Those alarm bells are negative behaviors triggered by the emotions we're not built to feel: anger, anxiety, frustration, fear, or doubt.

Learning to Follow Instructions

The Inner Voice principle of surrender means just that: surrender completely. Not surrender part of it, not surrender for a test period. Surrender all of it completely for all time.

I'm divorced, and I was going through some serious difficulties with my former wife regarding visitation with my teenage son. I loved him dearly but hadn't been allowed to see him for more than two years, even though I had been faithfully paying support. I had decided to give up my parental rights and simply walk away from my son—even though the real problem was with his mother.

Then I landed in the home of a friend who followed the Inner Voice way of life. I had gone there to visit my friend during his recovery from surgery, and I ended up doing a lot of healing myself. I shared what was happening in my life and told him my plans. His only comment was to ask if I minded if he told me about an experience he'd had with his daughter. After telling me that, he told me about surrender.

Later that evening, I tried a qualified version of the surrender technique during my nightly prayer to the creator. I felt somewhat at peace as I fell asleep. But during my morning prayer the next day, the creator spoke to me clearly: He told me to surrender it all to Him. Then He told me exactly what to do to. I was to call my former wife, tell her how much I cared about her (and I truly do care about her, even though our marriage didn't work), how much I loved my son, and that I would always be there for both of them.

I did as I was told. I called, and she listened without comment. Even though the conversation ended without a resolution, I was at peace. I had surrendered, and I wasn't going to try to take it back. My creator was in control.

And then a day later, she called and asked me to come see my son. Her words were music to my ears that brought tears to my eyes. I'm no longer even considering giving up my parental rights; I'll do everything I can to be the father—and the person—my creator wants me to be.

— Todd,
chief financial officer

When I experience an alarm bell, my first step is to figure out what's causing it. Am I out of today, stuck in yesterday, or trying to live in tomorrow? Am I trying to control someone or something that's out of my control? Am I feeling things I'm not meant to feel? Am I not as connected as I usually am to my inner voice?

Once I can name it, I surrender it.

If I find myself finger-pointing, judging, or blaming—that is, in self-pity or victim mode—and I can't see my part in what's making my alarm bells go off, I get on the phone and reach out to an Inner Voice coach or someone I know who's practicing Inner Voice principles. Every time I've done this, the person I called was able to help me, to talk me down from my proverbial ledge.

The more you practice Inner Voice principles and strategies, the easier it'll be for you to identify your own alarm bells. When they go off, don't ignore them. The faster you take action, the faster you can silence them and get back to living your purpose with the passion your creator intended.

It's Okay to Make Mistakes

I wish I could tell you that understanding your inner voice and making the decision to live the Inner Voice way of life will guarantee you a life that includes everything you want without problems, challenges, or discord. I admit that I don't know everything—but one thing I absolutely know for certain is that this is not the way it works.

Think of the inner voice as a rudder that turns a boat. The rudder only works if the boat is moving. If we turn the wrong way, as long as we're moving forward and taking action consistently, we can always correct the rudder and get back on track.

Once we learn how to make and maintain conscious contact with the inner voice, the right answer and right result will always come—as long as we don't quit. When we stop moving, we've quit.

CHAPTER EIGHT

To Build Your Passion, First Find Your Purpose

Why are we here on this earth?

It's a question that humans have been asking since the beginning of time. Some of us figure it out when we're young, some of us don't understand it until our middle-age or senior years, and some of us never get it. And often our answers to the "Why are we here?" question are superficial and incomplete. Yet until we get a meaningful answer, we waste a lot of time on actions that don't matter and negative emotions we shouldn't feel; we're running on the proverbial hamster wheel: going round and round, and expending a great deal of energy, but never getting anywhere.

Now that you have completed your first Discovery Chart and know how to practice two-way conscious contact, you have the tools you need to answer this question, to figure out the reason you were put on earth. Once you understand that, your passion will grow and you can develop and follow a plan to achieve your purpose.

As we begin this discussion on passion and purpose, I'm well aware that this phrase has become an overused cliché. A search of the phrase on Google generates more than 41 million results. But we keep talking about it, because it's important to us. We know we're not meant to drift aimlessly. We know we're not meant to hate or do harm. We know there's more to our beings than simple biology. But what is it, and how do we find it?

Let's begin our inner voice discussion of passion and purpose with definitions: Our *passion* is what we love to do; we need to understand not only what that is, but also why it is. Our *purpose* is our reason for being on this earth. It's what we were put here to do. It's our true meaning of life. It's not mysterious; it's not religious—it's simply our purpose.

Inner Voice Whispers

The most common reason for failure in life is not identifying your purpose and developing a plan to live it out.

Our purpose is a song most of us know we have to sing, but we're trying to figure out how. Inner Voice principles and strategies are the melody and lyrics to your song of purpose. When our passion and purpose come together in harmony, we can grow from being an individual instrument to an orchestra that becomes an unstoppable force of good.

The Fallacy of "Do What You Love and the Money Will Follow"

You've probably heard various versions of this advice: Figure out what you love to do (your passion), then figure out a way to make money doing that (your purpose), and the result will be that you'll live the life of your dreams and make plenty of money. That's warrior training, and the problem is that it's too simplistic and not always true.

The reality is that it often takes uncovering our purpose to unleash our passion. And our purpose is so much more than what we enjoy spending our time doing. You may enjoy cooking, but that doesn't mean food preparation should automatically be part of your plan to live out your purpose. You might enjoy a particular sport, but you're not necessarily meant to play it professionally. I've always loved to teach—and I'll talk more about how that's part of my purpose—but I don't have the required formal education to teach in traditional education environments such as elementary, primary, or secondary schools. There's also the consideration that teaching is one of the lowest-paid professions, and I prefer a more affluent lifestyle than most teachers can afford (no disrespect intended).

Another reality is that the idea of figuring out what you love to do and accepting that as your purpose is shallow. Your purpose is bigger than you are, and it's bigger than whatever work you choose to do. Better than figuring out what you want is to find out what God wants you to do so that you can live out your creator's purpose. That's where you'll find your passion and joy. Most of us can find that through the Discovery Chart, often tied into our childhood wounds and experiences.

When I was first making my mark in real estate as an investor, and in my early days of training others how to do what I was doing, people thought I had a passion for real estate investing. I didn't. When I bought that first book on how to make money in real estate, I didn't know anything about it; how could I have a passion for it? I was driven by a need to make money, because I believed that this was the way to show the people who'd told me I was no good and would never amount to anything that they were wrong. At the age of 20, when I stayed up all night reading a "get-rich" book, I was still years away from knowing my purpose—but I was absolutely

Inner Voice Whispers

Sometimes it takes struggles, losses, and misdirection to finally align with what we are meant to be doing at this point in life.

on the path my creator intended for me, and chances are good that you are, too. Here's where my passion began to reveal itself: My early real estate investments were run-down properties in low-income neighborhoods that I would buy, clean up, fix up, and rent out. It didn't take me long to realize that there was a serious need for safe, decent, clean, affordable housing for low-income people and that it was possible to build wealth by providing that housing. While I never had a passion for real estate per se (in particular, I didn't love doing the work of cleaning and fixing up those distressed properties), I developed a passion and a reputation for providing safe, decent, clean places for low- and moderate-income people to live. That passion for helping people was one of the key underlying messages of all my books and trainings on real estate investing and successful business creation.

Even today, after my various real estate investments (which have gone far beyond low-income housing to include commercial properties, middle- and upper-income residential properties, resorts, and more) have generated hundreds of millions of dollars in profits for me and my partners, I'm not necessarily passionate about real estate. I know how to do it, and I can make money at it; it just isn't what gives my life meaning. I am, however, passionate about what real estate lets me do, which is to live out the purpose my creator intended for me. And that purpose has evolved from providing excellent low-income housing to helping people discover their own purpose and passion so that they can live a life of peace, joy, and success.

I want to make an important distinction here: Even though real estate is not my passion, I enjoyed it. I enjoyed finding and analyzing the deals, identifying and overcoming the obstacles, and putting all the pieces together so that everybody won. We're not meant to spend our time doing things we don't enjoy, things that make us miserable. But living our purpose is a process that often includes doing things that don't rank as our passion but contribute to it.

What to Do When Nothing Else Works

I was a classic success story: founder of a multimillion-dollar business, a master networker who routinely rubbed shoulders with other millionaires and even a few billionaires, happily married, and a devout Christian.

My life began to unravel when my business failed. I couldn't figure out what I was doing wrong, why things weren't working as they used to. My marriage was stressed and my faith tested. I was fighting hard to make a comeback, but it seemed to be a losing battle.

I shared my frustrations with Russ Whitney, my Inner Voice coach. He taught me how to surrender: how to give my troubles up to God and let Him do what I can't.

Within 24 hours, I had received four amazing business offers. Five days later, I took over as CEO and president of a major company; it went from nothing to "done deal" in less than a week.

It was so miraculous and it happened so fast that if it hadn't happened to me, I wouldn't have believed it. But it was me, and I had to believe it because I was living it. My faith was restored, my marriage has recovered, and I'm on a new path of success and growth.

— Marc,

corporate executive

My purpose is to help people. My passion is teaching and sharing; I can help people by teaching them what I've learned that they can use to improve their lives and reach their goals. I was teaching even as far back as the years I spent in prison in my late teens; I helped other inmates learn to read and improve their comprehension skills. But I can't teach what I don't know. That means that in order to teach people how to build wealth through real estate and business, I had to learn it and do it myself—so I did. And to teach people how to live the life their creator intended using the inner voice, I had to learn it and do it myself. And I, like you, am a work in progress.

It's All in the Timing

I always knew that God had a plan for me, just as He has a plan for you. We've been training to execute that plan our entire lives—even when we didn't know what it was. Every experience, every twist and turn, every blessing, every tragedy, every struggle has put you and me right where we're supposed to be—even when it didn't seem like it at the time. When you use the Discovery Chart and other Inner Voice principles to connect the dots backward, you'll see this very clearly.

Inner Voice Whispers

If you don't like the problems in your life and in your world, stop giving so much of your attention to them. Instead of being sick and tired and upset about the way things are, be positively passionate about the way you would like things to be. Your life will instantly start to change for the better.

Your purpose is unique to you. Equally important is that it's not static. It changes and matures, and you change and mature. What may have been your purpose ten years ago could now be just a stepping-stone to your future greatness, purpose, and passion. Something else you need to know is that your purpose won't always appear to be safe and practical. It may generate the occasional twinge of fear—which is why you need passion to go with it.

Very often we don't develop our passion until we understand the role it takes in fulfilling our purpose. This is something I've seen over and over among those who follow the Inner Voice way of life: after they understood their purpose and began working on a plan to achieve it, they became passionate about something they'd never given any thought to before, because it was key to their purpose.

It's always valuable to ask yourself if your life's purpose matches your passion. If we can match our purpose with our passion and earn an honest living, we're on the road to great success—however we define success for ourselves. However, if you're feeling passionate about something but it isn't working for you, you may need to take a closer look. It may be that the universe is saying, "This door is closed."

Over the last five years, even as I've been developing the Inner Voice program, I've been involved in a number of other business ventures. Several would have delivered valuable financial education to people who could have used it to enhance their lives, but those opportunities just didn't work the way I thought they would. Although they weren't failures, they just weren't great successes. Through conscious contact with my inner voice, I've come to understand that those types of businesses aren't what I'm supposed to be doing at this stage of my life. The creator wants me working on sharing the Inner Voice way of life with as many people as possible, and I can't do that if I'm simultaneously working on unrelated businesses.

When something isn't working, great. It means the universe may be steering you in a different direction. Listen to your inner voice and follow the first pure thoughts.

Why Do Crises Happen?

Our lives will never be free of crises. It would be nice if we could do everything right and have nothing go wrong, but that's not the way it is. No matter how hard we try to avoid them, we'll have crises that we'll have to deal with. We'll get sick. People we've

Hitting Bottom Let Me Bounce Back Higher

My situation wasn't unique: I had a great job with a Fortune 500 company that paid a more-than-comfortable income and included an excellent benefits package. While my professional life looked perfect, my personal life was falling apart. I had separated from my wife after 25 years of marriage, I wasn't paying attention to or practicing my faith, and I wasn't taking care of myself physically. And then I got laid off.

My severance package was nice, but it didn't last long. And although I was exceptionally qualified for all the jobs I applied for, I wasn't hired. I was out of money, energy, and options when a friend I hadn't seen in years heard about what was happening with me and called. He wasn't offering a job or a loan; he wanted to share the Inner Voice.

The Discovery Chart showed me how much fear, anxiety, frustration, self-doubt, and anger I was experiencing. Even so, I resisted the idea that I was powerless and needed to surrender; what I needed was a job, and I'd be fine, thank you very much.

My friend never lost patience with me—and he didn't give up on me. I gradually realized that I'm indeed powerless over other people and things, and that when I tried to control things I couldn't control, my life became unmanageable. I was feeling hate and resentment, wanting to strike out and get revenge.

Where was that getting me? Only to a place of self-pity, darkness, and regret.

LIVING THE INNER VOICE LIFE, CONT.

What were my options? Surrender.

When I finally surrendered, I had the best cry of my life. I asked for clarity and received it. Today I'm on a totally different path than in my corporate days. I have a new career doing something I truly love, my faith has been restored, I'm physically healthy, and I'm in a wonderful relationship with an amazing woman.

— Stewart,
entrepreneur

never harmed will harm us. We'll have accidents. But in every crisis is an opportunity to grow; it's one of the immutable laws of the universe.

In my experience, crisis shows up in our lives for one or a combination of these four reasons:

- We have a character defect that we need to fix.

- We have a behavior that we need to change or improve.

- We have a vice that we need to give up.

- We're not stepping up to our potential; we're not meeting the purpose we're supposed to meet at this point in our life.

You can have any or all of these issues going on in your life and not have a crisis for a while. The universe will give you a chance to take care of things on your own. But when you don't, the universe will nudge you.

What makes a crisis bigger or smaller in our lives is the resistance we give to it. If we yield and correct the defect, change the behavior, give up the vice, or step up, the crisis diminishes and goes away. If we go into victim mode, wringing our hands and crying, "Why me?" the crisis will get bigger and bigger.

The best way to deal with a crisis is to listen to your inner voice. Don't whine and don't complain. Simply ask what you're supposed to be doing and do it. Chances are your inner voice has been trying to give you that message and you haven't heard it because your human self is blocking it.

Am I suggesting that we deserve the bad things that happen to us? Not at all. But life is a struggle—not a nonstop struggle, but a struggle. That's the way it's supposed to be. If it wasn't, we'd have no reason to be more patient, no reason to be more kind, no reason to be more tolerant, no reason to let go of resentments, and certainly no reason to be better people today than we were yesterday. Remember this: The gift of life is in the struggle, and the gift of the struggle is discovering the answer to the question, "What is the lesson?"

Inner Voice Whispers

Find inspiration in failure. When something isn't working, it means the universe is steering you in a different direction. It's telling you to take a different action and produce a new result.

The lesson isn't that we're victims. It's not about self-pity or "woe is me." It's about how the struggle made us stronger, better, wiser. It's about how the struggle prepares us for what's to come. Let me share a story one of my early coaches told me that helped me understand the concept of our struggles being gifts.

A man was walking through a forest when he stumbled upon a cocoon that contained a chrysalis (the pupal stage of butterflies). The cocoon had fallen to the ground, and the man could see that a butterfly was struggling to get out of it. The kind man took out his pocketknife and made an incision into the cocoon, cutting a hole just big enough for the morphing butterfly to escape and be free. The grateful butterfly squeezed through the hold, soared for about 30 feet, and then fell to the ground and died. Why? Because morphing butterflies need the struggle of pushing against the cocoon to build up the strength they need to survive in the world. Although the well-intentioned man thought he was helping, the reality was that not letting the butterfly have its struggle led to the creature's early death.

As humans, we don't have to break free of physical cocoons, but we need to struggle to build our strength and fulfill our purpose. We should look forward to struggles, not run away from them. With any struggle comes a door that opens to something better. When you try to avoid struggles, you are cheating yourself out of the best that life has to offer.

Inner Voice Whispers

When you know your purpose, your passion will build naturally over time.

Should Perfection Be Your Goal?

I don't believe our creator intended us to be error free; in fact, I know that making mistakes is how we grow, learn, and improve. We're not expected to do anything perfect the first time; we are, however, expected to make progress as we go along, to try to be just a little better today than we were yesterday.

Something else about perfection to consider is this: What is perfection? Who decides if something is perfect? If you're living your purpose according to the plan of your creator, you're living perfectly. You'll make mistakes. You'll experience failure. And from those mistakes and failures, you'll figure out what didn't work and take a new action to produce a new result. It's part of your purpose. However, even though perfection by human standards doesn't necessarily have to be your goal, something else does: Living according to "HOW."

∞

CHAPTER NINE

LIVING BY HOW

Even though our world is governed by the immutable laws of the universe—laws that we can't change—we still have a lot of choices we can make for ourselves about our lives and relationships. One of the most powerful life principles I can share with you is *HOW*. It stands for the following:

- Honesty
- Open-mindedness
- Willingness

This principle is fundamental to the Inner Voice way of life. It's the proverbial three-legged stool: when any part is incomplete or missing, the stool will, at best, wobble and, at worst, fall over. Here's how I learned to live by HOW.

Honesty

When I left the retreat in Hawaii, I hired José, who had been on staff at the facility, to travel with me for several months. I told you about José earlier; he was the Latin fellow who initially convinced me to stay at the retreat when I first arrived and was determined to leave. He's a good coach with a lot of experience, and my reputation didn't intimidate him at all. In fact, I think he might have been tougher on me than he was when working with people who had less forceful personalities than I do.

We left the island of Oahu and went to a resort on Maui. One night, José and I were sitting on the balcony of the hotel overlooking the ocean while he worked with me on understanding and developing statesperson (soul self) character assets, when my cell phone rang. It was a friend from Florida who hadn't seen or heard from me in a while, and she was wondering where I had disappeared to. I told that her I was in Hawaii, that I was planning on going from there to Fiji, and that I wouldn't be back in Florida for at least a month. That was only partially true. Although I was in Hawaii and didn't expect to be back in Florida for a while, I wasn't going to Fiji. I had thought about it, but changed my plans and was heading to California instead to see another friend as part of my quest to find my life's true purpose.

Inner Voice
Whispers

The big decisions, the ones you pay a lot of attention to, will set the direction for your life. However, the small decisions are what deliver and maintain that direction.

After chatting with my Florida friend for a few more minutes, I ended the call. I put down my phone and turned to José, who was looking at me with an expression of total disgust. He clicked his tongue to make a noise that I recognized as meaning that he wasn't happy. I wasn't quite sure what he was disturbed about, so I ignored it and prepared to go back to our discussion on character assets. José clicked his tongue again and gave me another look of disgust. Now I was disturbed, so I asked him what his problem was.

Very humbly, he said, "Russ, it's time now for us to start working on your honesty."

My immediate response was to challenge him. "What are you talking about?"

"It's time to start working on your honesty," he said again.

I challenged him again. "What are you talking about? I'm an honest person. What's wrong with you?"

Softly but firmly, he said, "If you are honest, why did you tell that person you're going to Fiji? You aren't going to Fiji; you're going to California."

For a moment, he had me; but then I rebounded with what I thought was a good reason for not telling my Florida friend the truth. "People are always following me where I go and trying to keep tabs on me. I like to have some anonymity in my life and some breathing room."

"That's very nice, Russ, and I understand," José said. He paused long enough for me to think I'd satisfied his question and disposed of his suggestion that I needed to work on honesty; then he asked, "So, if you'll lie about that, what else will you lie about?"

Ouch!

José told me to think about it and gave me an assignment of making an inventory of how many times I lied during an average day. He defined *lie* as anything that wasn't completely true, from a total falsehood to a mild exaggeration.

It was another Inner Voice Awakening—this time, a huge one. There's no argument that things such as violating marriage vows and stealing are dishonest. But have you ever told your boss or anyone else that you were late because of traffic, when in fact you just didn't get up in time or were doing something else you didn't want to stop? Have you ever told the dry cleaner you needed your clothes back that night because you were leaving town in the morning, but in fact you weren't? If you're a business owner or manager, did you ever implement a policy that wasn't effective and then try to give "credit" for the idea (make that "blame") to someone else when you realized your idea was terrible? And here's one more question: Do you do things when no one's looking that you wouldn't do if you could be seen?

It's important to understand that there's honesty—and there's brutal honesty. We shouldn't be brutal; we shouldn't let honesty hurt God, us, or another human being. Always temper the truth with kindness, but always be honest. For example, you might be thinking that there are times when "little white lies" are appropriate, such as that age-old "Does this dress make me look fat?" question or when you feel that the truth would be hurtful. That's simply not true. Certainly you want to couch what you say in ways that are kind, but it should always be the truth. You don't have to say, "Yes, that dress makes you look like a blimp." You could say, "I think the style of your blue dress is more flattering to your figure." Dishonesty, no matter what the reason or motivation, is a serious character defect.

As I came to terms with this, I began to understand what was behind this character defect in me. As I've said, when I was a child, I never knew what was going to happen to me when I got home from school every day. I didn't know if I would be greeted with a smile or a kick or a punch. I could do things that would be ignored one day but spark a beating the next. My stepmother would ask me a question, and if she didn't get the "right" answer, I would suffer for it. The problem was that the "right" answer didn't always have to be the truth; it just had to be what she wanted to hear that day. When I did my Discovery Chart, I came to understand that I had learned to lie to try to avoid being hurt, and it was a habit that I had carried into adulthood. I didn't think there was anything wrong with it, because my goal wasn't to hurt anyone else; it was often quite the opposite.

Getting hit over the head with the honesty lesson that evening in Hawaii was one of the best things that ever happened to me. I began living my life in a totally new way—not only being honest with others, but also, more important, being honest with myself. It was an amazing life change for me. I admit it wasn't always comfortable or easy, but it was always best. And as I continued to study and grow, I learned that the people who consistently function in the statesperson phase, in touch with their soul selves, consistently put honesty at the top of their priorities.

The response I get from the people I coach is always very close to mine. They're amazed and gratified at the difference that total honesty makes in their lives: being honest with others, honest with God, and honest with themselves. As I was walking one of my clients through this lesson and asked if she'd ever used traffic as a false excuse for not being somewhere on time, she started laughing. "Russ, I keep a picture of a traffic accident on my cell phone, and I've sent it to people when I was running late," she said. Although she laughed, she was genuinely horrified. She quickly understood the seriousness of the issue and that what she thought was a clever way to get away with something was, in fact, a fundamental character defect.

Honesty is the first principle that we must practice daily. It's the first one we should try to perfect. It's our initial commitment to the Inner Voice way of life, and it's tremendously freeing.

Open-Mindedness

The next part of the principle of HOW is open-mindedness. We have to be open-minded enough to recognize that maybe, just maybe, there's another way to approach life to get the best from it and help other people along the way.

Being open-minded doesn't mean accepting everything you hear or following someone in a sheeplike way. Even as you are open-minded, you must also be discerning. It's okay to ask questions and seek clarification. Remember that part of the process of two-way conscious contact is to test the answer to confirm that it's actually coming from your inner voice and not your human self. As you start to implement the Inner Voice principles and strategies, I urge you to look for

Inner Voice Whispers

Stop needing the approval of others, and you'll receive more approval and support than ever. Live each moment from your own inspiration, not from a desire to look good in the eyes of others.

evidence that they're working. And if and when you reject something, be sure you're doing it for valid reasons.

LIVING THE INNER VOICE LIFE

The Truth Really Does Set You Free

I remember the thump, the sound of me hitting a
state of absolute bewilderment. I was at the bottom,
and I was alone—more alone than I'd ever been. I had
lost my wife, my family, my business, my partner's trust,
and probably a lot of other things I couldn't identify. I
was certain that everything that was wrong in my life
was someone else's fault.

That's when I reconnected with a friend who
introduced me to the inner voice. Some of the things I
heard hurt at first, because it was painful to admit who
I was. I tried to do the honesty test of keeping a log
of the lies I told for just 24 hours. I couldn't finish it; I
was too embarrassed. I didn't realize how dishonest I
actually was.

Learning and applying the Inner Voice principles
and strategies has meant freedom for me: the freedom
to rebuild my life, my marriage, and my business. I'm
not perfect, but every day I spend less time in the valley.
I love that I'm challenged daily to grow into the person
my God wants me to be.

— Benjamin,
investor, entrepreneur

The creator talks to each of us differently at different times.
Sometimes we hear specific words. Sometimes thoughts just pop
into our heads. Sometimes the message comes from a book or from
something someone says. Sometimes we see things that send us a

visual message. Sometimes we just know what the creator is trying to tell us without understanding how we know it. And sometimes we need to accept the fact that the creator may not be ready to give us an answer.

Here's how I learned this: I have a room in my house that you might call a chapel or meditation room. It's designed to honor all spiritual beliefs, not just one formal religion. It includes a cross that, for construction reasons, had to be slightly offset in a way such that it casts an interesting shadow. One morning several years ago, I was on my way to a meeting. It was very foggy, and visibility was extremely limited. I was troubled about something and working on surrendering it. I could barely see 100 feet in front of my car as I started to cross a bridge, but when I reached the peak of the bridge, the sun popped out shining as brightly as could be for about 30 seconds, and then it disappeared again. On the sun appeared to be a cross, slightly offset, just as the cross in my chapel is. When I saw that cross, I knew it was the creator telling me that I was being heard and that the answer would come when I needed it, as long as I stayed open and receptive.

On another occasion, I was struggling with trying to find an answer to a personal situation I needed to deal with. I'd been tied up in knots about it for a couple of weeks. My house is on the water, and I was sitting on my dock, thinking about my dilemma. I thought I had an answer, but I wasn't sure if it was right or if I really wanted to do it. Part of me was surrendering, and part of me was whining. As I was talking to the creator, two gorgeous ten-foot dolphins swam by the dock. I see dolphins from my house all the time, but this was different. There were two of them, swimming in tandem, and they were beautiful. At that moment, feeling desperate, I said, "God, if you want me to do X about this situation, make one of those dolphins jump out of the water." I knew it was a ridiculous request (then again, maybe it wasn't) for a lot of reasons, not the least of which was that in all the years I'd lived on the water, and of all the dolphins I'd seen swimming close to the houses, I'd never seen one jump there. But this time, I heard a whoosh, and one of the dolphins jumped out of the water. I realized that I had my answer, and I knew what I had to do.

Since then, I have had hundreds of similar experiences—not with dolphins jumping, of course, but with small, subtle, and some not-so-subtle signs that the answer I needed was coming and would come when the time was right.

Here's another story: I was working at home, thinking I was doing a good job of living in the present, when I heard a dog barking. The barking was loud and persistent, coming from the house next door. To the best of my knowledge, my neighbors didn't have a dog, so this either was a new pet or a visiting one; in either case, it was distracting me, and I couldn't focus on my work. After a while, unable to concentrate, I decided to go outside and nicely ask my neighbors to quiet the dog so that I could get my work done. As I walked around my house to theirs, a big, clumsy creature came galloping toward me with a ball in his mouth. He dropped the ball at my feet, "smiled" at me, and barked. I couldn't resist; I threw the ball. He chased it and brought it back. It turned out that the dog belonged to some friends who were visiting my neighbors, and I ended up spending most of the day outside playing with him and talking with my neighbors. It was a beautiful, sunny day, and we all had a wonderful time. When I finally went back into my house, I was able to quickly and effectively accomplish the work I'd been trying to do earlier, when I'd first heard the dog. I believe that dog was a message from God, telling me to get outside, relax, and enjoy His creation. It's just one more example of how the creator speaks to us differently at different times, based on where we are and what we need.

Not long after I had that experience of seeing the dolphin jump out of the water, a friend of mine was visiting from out of state. He was going through a tough time, and I was doing my best to help on multiple levels, including sharing Inner Voice principles and discussing some business possibilities. He was skeptical. On the day he was scheduled to leave, the weather up north was bad, and his flight was delayed. He roamed around the Fort Myers airport, thinking about the things we'd discussed, trying to decide what to do. Staring out a window at a puddle, he recalled my story of the dolphins, and he began to pray: "God, I know you're not going to make a dolphin jump out of that puddle on the tarmac, but I'm in a very difficult place right now. If this inner voice stuff is real, please show me something." When he turned around, the first thing he saw was a fountain with a sculpture of three dolphins jumping out of the water. He snapped a picture with his cell phone and sent it to me. Coincidence? I don't think so. I invited him to come back to my house, where we began moving forward with our business deal and he became a passionate student of the Inner Voice way of life.

LIVING THE INNER VOICE LIFE

Ending the Blame Game

I was angry with a friend, certain that she was the cause of the problems in our relationship. During a heated argument, I pointed my finger at her and almost immediately recalled the Inner Voice lesson: When I'm pointing one finger at someone else, three more are pointing back at me.

Regardless of what she'd done or not done, I wasn't without fault. We called a temporary truce. The next morning, during my two-way conscious contact, I realized that the shortcomings she had that were upsetting me were shortcomings I had as well. I was actually angry with myself, not her. I'm using my inner voice to turn those nonproductive character defects into pleasing character assets. She graciously accepted my apology, and our friendship is stronger than ever.

— Wes,
chief operating officer

Someone once told me that the difference between knowledge and wisdom is this: Knowledge is book smarts and wisdom is what you've learned from experience. Knowledge doesn't do you a whole lot of good if you don't have wisdom. And it doesn't matter how smart you are or what you've achieved in life; you can always learn something from just about everyone you encounter. The key is to be open-minded enough to hear the wisdom when you have the opportunity.

Inner Voice Whispers

Life can throw us some mean curveballs. The gift and our success come from how we handle those tough times.

We must train ourselves to keep an open mind, to carefully consider things before we accept or reject them. We must open our eyes, look at the world differently, and be aware of the signs that could come from places we least expect with the answers we need. And we must be honest with ourselves when we slip back into our old ways and make decisions or take actions based on closed mindedness.

Willingness

The third part of the HOW principle is about action; you must be willing to do what it takes to live out your purpose as you build your passion. You must be willing to get out of your comfort zone, go on a daily search for the truth, and start making positive changes. It might feel awkward and uncomfortable at first, but when you see evidence and get results, you'll know you have a gift that many will never receive.

A key way that you can demonstrate willingness is with your two-way conscious contact. Look at what you've written down and do it; it really is that simple. My goal is to do everything that my inner voice tells me each day. No, I don't always succeed, but I do the best I can. After all, there's no point in asking my inner voice for direction if I'm going to ignore it, is there? And I know that my inner voice will remind me if I don't do something that's important.

Something I've learned that helps me with willingness is this: the creator is extraordinarily generous with gifts, but often there are things we need to do so that we're fully prepared to receive those gifts. Would you give your teenager a car if he hadn't learned how to drive? Of course not; you'd insist that your teen take driver's education and practice driving so that he would be prepared to drive before you gave him a car. If I have written down a message that's telling me to take a particular action, tested it to be sure it's from my creator, and then don't do it, I probably won't get the next gift that's meant for me, because I won't be prepared for it. I've learned that I can't expect the next gift if I don't follow the last command—and that's a good thing. So to make sure that I stay willing and act on my willingness, I regularly review my two-way conscious contact journal to be sure I've acted on all the answers I've received. If I find something I haven't acted on, I make it a part of my initial two-way conscious contact prayer for the present day. That way I can have what amounts to an updated message with clarification if I need it.

Inner Voice Whispers

Your greatest value comes from being who you truly are. Let your beautiful, unique, fascinating, and authentic self come out.

One of the beautiful aspects of willingness is how it ties into the time clock of life and why we should only live in the present. When you take action, you take action only for today. Don't worry about tomorrow until it gets here. You only have to do whatever your inner voice is telling you to do today. The creator never demands perfection, just progress. But progress requires daily effort and action.

The HOW Principle in Warrior Mode

An interesting thing about HOW is that many people have been taught to operate this way while they're still in their warrior phase. One of the great thought leaders that I've always had tremendous respect for and learned a lot from is the late Jim Rohn, who was a world-renowned business philosopher and recognized leader in the fields of motivation and personal achievement, as well as one of America's foremost authorities on success. Jim frequently talked about the four ingredients that lead to life change: disgust, decision, desire, and resolve. For many years, I taught a version of that to my wealth-building students: disgust, decision, and action.

I was unknowingly teaching the HOW principle for warriors: First, you become absolutely disgusted with your situation, whatever it happens to be. It could be financial, business, or personal. But you finally get to the point where you say, "Enough. I am disgusted with this, and I'm not going to tolerate this anymore." That's honesty for the statesperson. Second, you decide what you're going to do, and you put together a plan. That's open-mindedness for the statesperson. Third, you take action—the most important ingredient for change. That's willingness for the statesperson.

Even if you're still in warrior mode but you've been a student of personal development, you might find adopting Inner Voice principles and strategies easier than you thought it would be, because it's possible that you're already practicing the HOW principle.

Should You Fake It Till You Make It?

Although the phrase "Fake it till you make it" is contemporary, the concept has been around a long time. Aristotle put it this way: "Men acquire a particular quality by constantly acting a particular way. We become just by performing just actions, temperate by performing temperate actions, brave by performing brave actions."

The word *fake* gives me pause, because it carries the connotation of dishonesty. But there's a difference between being dishonest and acting in a way that may not yet be completely natural for us but that's clearly desirable. For example, I've long believed in the value of adopting a positive attitude and of acting and speaking in a positive way even if I don't genuinely feel that way. It was something I learned the hard way and shared in my book *Building Wealth:*

> We believe what we say. When we respond to greetings with a mumbled "I'm doing okay" or "I can't complain," we will build a life that fits that description. And if all you want is a life where you're getting along without anything to gripe about, just keep on talking this way. If you want to make yourself sicker, talk about your aches and pains. If you want to have a bad day, talk about the negatives.
>
> After I started my first business and had to hire people to work for me, I realized that negativity affected my *employees'* productivity. I decided that since I had found books that told me how to make money, maybe I could find some on how to have a better attitude. I bought one of those rah-rah positive-attitude books, and I hated every page of it. I thought it was the stupidest thing I'd ever read. Why? Because the author said that to become positive, you have to go around saying things like *super* and *fantastic*—words that were not in my everyday vocabulary. Not only did the technique seem phony, but I wasn't about to embarrass myself or put my oversized young ego on the line doing something I thought was silly.
>
> But my desire to become a millionaire soon overcame my ego. And if being positive and saying dumb things would help me reach my goal, then I'd give it a try.
>
> It was one of the hardest things I've ever done.
>
> Two interesting things happened. First, worker productivity increased significantly. I was delighted, because that meant more profits. Second, and even more important, I began liking myself when I was wearing my positive mask.

It wasn't long before I realized I had experienced a metamorphosis. I had unwittingly transformed myself from someone who was totally committed to negativity to someone who was positive, happy, and on a continuous search for bright things and the overall good in life.

My point in sharing this story is that it's not dishonest to act like you who want to be, especially when your behavior is demonstrating the character assets you want to develop. Essentially, that's practice for self-improvement. You're working on changing and improving from the inside out, not just putting on a façade. Acting is only dishonest if your intention is to deceive people.

Here's an example: One of the character defects I had to work on when I began living the Inner Voice way of life was being inconsiderate. As much as I'd have liked to, I couldn't flip a switch and become 100 percent considerate overnight. I had years of human training and habits to overcome. Although I was able to change many of my inconsiderate behaviors fairly quickly, sometimes I had to act considerate even when it wasn't what I really wanted to do. Better that I "faked" being considerate when I didn't totally feel that way than to be inconsiderate.

So should you fake it till you make it? You answer the question.

CHAPTER TEN

How Are You Doing?

Now that you've learned some of the Inner Voice fundamentals, how do you know that the program is working? When you go on a diet, you measure your progress by tracking your weight and your body-mass index. When you're learning a new skill, you measure your progress by tracking your speed and overall proficiency. When you're building financial independence, you measure your progress by tracking cash on hand and net worth. And when you're learning how to live the Inner Voice way of life, you measure your progress by making a daily inventory of your character assets and behaviors.

One of my first experiences with using an inventory was when José gave me the task of keeping track of how many times I was untruthful with myself or others during a day so that we could work on my own honesty. That exercise was an eye-opener in more ways than one. Besides giving me data that would help me work on my own personal character defect, it reinforced the importance of measuring our progress as we integrate Inner Voice principles and strategies into our lives.

I have worked with our Inner Voice team to develop a measurement system that's effective without being cumbersome. The Inner Voice Character Assets Checklist and Weekly Analysis chart at the back of the book combine a quick daily inventory with weekly analysis and planning. (You can also go to www.Inner Voice.com/book to download a full-sized version of the chart.)

At the end of every day, pull out your chart and rate your behavior for that day using a simple scale of *O* and *X*, with *O* signifying that you're doing well or making progress, and *X* indicating that you need improvement in this area. This shouldn't take more than a couple of minutes. I like to do this just before going to bed; it seems like a good way to close the day.

At the end of the week, look at your overall ratio of O's and X's to see how you're doing. It's not necessary to count so that you have specific totals; you can just look at your chart and see whether you have more O's, which means you're doing well, or more X's, which means you have issues that need work. The chart is designed to give you an instant view of your trends. Try it for a week and you'll see what I mean. Then go to the second page of the chart and list the top three areas in which you've made progress and the top three areas in which you need improvement. Now, think about what you did to make progress and what you need to do to improve, and then craft a brief action plan for the coming week.

Let's go through this together.

> *Inner Voice Whispers*
>
> If you want things to get better, you have to get better. If you want things to change, you have to change. You have to grow!

Character Assets Checklist

Listed are 19 character assets or behaviors for you to rank. This is by no means an exhaustive list, but it covers most of the issues you're likely to want and need to work on. I wanted to keep the approach positive, so this list doesn't include character defects; however, the defect would simply be the behavior that's opposite to the asset.

Your daily inventory is a lot like an inkblot test: your first impression is generally all you need. That's why it won't require a lot of time. Let's go through each asset and talk about the kinds of questions you can ask yourself.

- **Conscious contact with Inner Voice.** Did you do your two-way conscious-contact exercise or, in some other way, have deliberate, planned contact with your inner voice?

- **Honest with self.** Have you been honest with yourself, or have you tried to make excuses for things you've said, done, or thought?

- **Honest with others.** Have your words and actions been true, or have you told outright lies or distortions or been dishonest by omission?

- **Open-minded.** Have you taken the time to consider new ideas, or have you shut them down without any research or reflection?

- **Nonjudgmental.** Have you passed judgment on others, or have you left that process to God (or the God of your understanding)?

- **Complimentary, give credit, praise to others.** Have you made it a point to say nice things to others? Have you praised others for specific actions and, when appropriate, acknowledged and given credit for specific efforts? Or have you failed to give credit where it's due or, worse, taken credit for something someone else did?

- **Discreet, respect confidences.** Have you kept the secrets with which you were entrusted and resisted any temptation to gossip? Or have you revealed confidences or unnecessarily repeated unkind things?

- **Polite, courteous, considerate.** Have you used good manners and behaved in a way that's thoughtful and respectful of others? Or have you been rude and inconsiderate?

139

- **Humble.** Have you practiced humility? Or have you behaved arrogantly?

- **Grateful, not envious or jealous.** Do you regularly express gratitude for your gifts? Have you been happy for other people when they have what you want, or have you felt resentful and covetous?

- **Moderate, not gluttonous.** In all aspects of life, not just food, have you engaged in moderation rather than gluttony?

- **Initiative, not lazy, not procrastinating.** Have you taken action when necessary, or have you been idle and indolent? Have you done things on schedule that needed to be done, or have you put them off?

- **Unselfish, generous.** Have you shared yourself and your resources with others, not just by giving money but by being there for people who need you? Or have you been selfish and hoarded your gifts?

- **Trusting.** Have you taken people at their word, trusting them until and unless they prove to be untrustworthy? Or have you been unnecessarily suspicious?

- **Forgiving.** Have you forgiven others for any real or perceived offenses? Equally important, have you forgiven yourself for your mistakes? Or are you harboring grudges and resentments that are hurting you more than the target of your feelings?

- **Sincere, straightforward, not manipulative.** Have you been genuine and truthful in your dealings, or have you said or done things you didn't mean? Have you been candid and open about your wants and needs, or have you used devious techniques to get others to do your bidding?

- **Act with integrity and responsibility.** Do you demonstrate integrity by doing the right thing simply because it's the right thing to do? Have you accepted responsibility for your thoughts and actions, or have you blamed others?

- **Kind, nice, not sarcastic.** Have you treated others pleasantly, in a way that wouldn't be cutting or insulting?

- **Positive, optimistic.** Do you express a positive attitude and consistently look at the upside of situations? Or are you expecting the worst to happen?

Once you've gone through the list and marked your chart, look it over and pick out one or two things you could work on the next day, and ask for help with that when you do your morning two-way conscious contact. Then put your inventory aside until the next evening, when it's time to do it again.

Weekly Analysis

Although simply taking a daily inventory can be powerful, it's even better if you use that information to make conscious improvements in your life. Schedule a weekly meeting with yourself to review your Character Assets Checklist and decide what to do with that information. The chart at the back of the book begins on Sunday, but you should do your weekly analysis on whatever day works best for you. It will be more effective if you pick a day and time that's convenient, and stick to a schedule.

When you list the areas in which you've made progress, give some thought to what you did to achieve that so that you can continue doing it. For the areas in which you need improvement, think about what's holding you back. You may need to revisit your Discovery Chart for help.

Your action plan and notes to yourself can be as simple or complex as you feel you need. I suggest keeping it simple, because

I Didn't Take That Call—and the World Is Still Turning!

I was a cell phone addict and workaholic. I was on my phone all the time; I never let it out of my sight. And it didn't matter what I was doing or who I was with; when my phone rang, I took the call. At parties, out to dinner with friends, on vacation, my business came first.

After a while, I realized I wasn't getting as many social invitations. It finally dawned on me that my friends didn't want to be around me, because even when I was with them, I wasn't really there. I was seriously out of balance and had fooled myself into thinking I was being productive.

My Inner Voice coach helped me understand that God doesn't honor anything that keeps us out of balance, as my workaholism and phone addiction were doing to me. He said, "No matter how hard you try, you're not going to make a deal that isn't supposed to happen. If it's meant to be, you can handle it during regular business hours. Yes, I understand that there may be times when you need to work into the evening or take an early-morning call, but as an everyday rule, use a sound life-balance ratio of work to recreation."

I had already successfully applied other Inner Voice principles, so I asked my inner voice to give me the direction I needed to restore balance to my life. Today, I get more done in less time and enjoy a rich social life, with people I enjoy who enjoy me. And if I miss a call, no big deal. They'll either leave a message or call back.

— Meghan,
owner, marketing and design studio

if you make it complicated, you'll be less like to consistently do it. You should also make it achievable. Don't commit to losing ten pounds in a week; that's not achievable or healthy. Don't commit to donating 30 hours of volunteer time if you're already juggling a full-time job and a family. Think about what you can realistically do to improve, to move toward changing your character defects to assets. You might need to commit to watching your language or being more punctual. You might include a note to call someone you haven't spoken with in a while, to volunteer to do something for your favorite cause, or even to begin the process of mending a broken relationship. You might make a note to remember to practice surrender sooner rather than later, before an issue mushrooms from a small problem to a massive conflict.

Inner Voice Whispers

Take an inventory of yourself today. Pick two things you can change or do better. Work on those two things just for today.

After you do your first weekly analysis, compare your current week to previous weeks to see your progress and make sure you've implemented your action plan. Even though your goal is to make steady progress, don't be too hard on yourself if you find yourself needing improvement in an area this week that you were doing well in last week. Instead, use your two-way conscious contact to identify the issue and get it resolved. Don't let your mind get cluttered with guilt, shame, rationalization, or justification. Remember the game of life: When the day is over, it's over. Surrender it. The score is the score; you can't change it— and when you start tomorrow, you start with a clean slate and clear scoreboard.

Losing It All Made Me a Winner

I was spoiled. I wanted things my way, and I'd had enough business success that I could be a tyrant if anyone had the gall to argue with me. But that kind of success is fragile, and eventually my life started falling apart. My business ventures failed, I was in a toxic romantic relationship, I was estranged from my children, I was overweight and out of shape—and then I got cancer. That was the final straw; I couldn't deal with it anymore. I began contemplating suicide.

Then a friend told me about the inner voice. It sounded good, but I wasn't sure. So I asked God for a sign—and got it immediately. I began studying and practicing two-way conscious contact.

A year later, I have a wonderful relationship with my kids, I'm out of the toxic romantic relationship, I've lost weight, and I'm rebuilding my business. Even better is that I'm no longer a bully or a dictator; I have healthy relationships with people who like me for who I am, not for what I have or what I can do for them.

— Allen,
real estate investor

Write It Down

A key part of the inventory process is using the Character Assets Checklist and writing it down. This isn't effective if you try to do it in your head. For me, and for the Inner Voice members I've discussed this with, what makes the inventory work is actually marking the page with the *X*'s and *O*'s, and then looking at the trend at the end of each week.

Brandon has been living the Inner Voice way of life for several years. He's done his Discovery Chart and practices two-way conscious contact every day. He figured he had it covered and didn't need to do the inventory. Then one day, during his two-way conscious contact, this message came: "Do your Character Assets Checklist." He heard it but decided to ignore it because he was too busy. A week later, the message came again. This time, he listened. "I started doing it, and it really started working for me," he said. "I take my inventory every day and do the analysis once a week. When you write it down, you realize you might not be as on track as you thought you were, but that's okay, because you know what you need to work on, you can fix the things that need fixing, and you can see your progress. Doing the Character Assets Checklist according to the program has made a huge difference for me."

The Only Checklist We Do Is for Ourselves

The Inner Voice community is extraordinarily caring and sharing, and when you become a part of it, you'll likely want to share what you're learning. Wonderful! But even as I say that, let me issue this caution: Resist the urge to do a Character Assets Checklist for someone else. It's not your job to tell others that they are or aren't being honest, or that they're being arrogant rather than humble. Even though your assessment may be accurate, keep it to yourself. Share from your own experience, strength, and hope.

An Inner Voice member I was coaching was working on surrendering and forgiving a wrong that had been done to her. In the process, she talked about understanding why the other person had done what he'd done, about the things in his past that had caused the character defects that contributed to his behavior. She felt that expressing an understanding of what drove his selfish and dishonest actions was important to enable her to forgive; it's not. That's conditional forgiveness, and it's judgmental, which is a character defect. Keeping track of our own character assets and defects is a big enough job by itself; we don't need to worry about doing it for others.

Doing a Character Assets Checklist for someone else is a form of finger-pointing and judging. And every time you point a finger at someone else, three more fingers are pointing back at you.

Start with Baby Steps

Two key guidelines for using the Character Assets Checklist are:

- Give yourself credit for your improvements.
- Don't try to fix everything at once.

The Character Assets Checklist will clearly show you where you're off track—but it will also show you where you're on track, what you're doing well. Celebrate that!

Inner Voice
Whispers

Getting started is better than getting nothing.

No matter how many "needs improvement" marks you see on your chart, don't try to tackle everything at once. Pick one or two, three at the most, areas that are the most offensive to you that day, and make a commitment to work on them the next day. Remember that the Inner Voice way of life means that we live in the present, not yesterday or tomorrow. So you only have to work on your behaviors one day at a time. You only have to do what you can do. Start with baby steps, and your journey will take care of itself.

CHAPTER ELEVEN

A DAY IN THE INNER
VOICE WAY OF LIFE

In my warrior years, I was routinely up before dawn and worked well into the night. I frequently wasn't able to sleep, because my mind and thoughts were all stuck in tomorrow and in the false land of "what if." When this happened, I would either go into my home office or drive over to the company office, where I would work until the sun came up and my schedule for the day began. My business associates and employees were very accustomed to receiving e-mails from me with a time stamp of two, three, or four o'clock in the morning. My extended business day was always booked—and often double-booked—with meetings. Lunches and dinners, if I took them at all, were meant for business discussions. For years, I rarely took a lunch break. I'd work through the lunch hour, and if I did eat, it was in my office. If people I was meeting with got hungry, I'd insist on a working lunch in my office. And still I felt as if I couldn't get everything done.

Today, I often still get up before dawn, because I like being awake in those early-morning hours; it's a beautiful time of day. I use that time, when no one is around and the phone isn't ringing, to engage in my two-way conscious contact with my inner voice. And although my days are generally full, I don't double-book; I allow plenty of time for meetings so that no one is shortchanged or inconvenienced, and I rarely work in the evenings. I practice the Inner Voice principle of being in the moment. Most of my meals are times to relax and enjoy the company of family and friends. Although I still have business lunches and dinners, I make sure that they're relaxing and that they provide a break from the work at hand. At the end of most days, I know that I've done everything I was supposed to do—or at least that it was all I could do and stay in the moment for that day. What a beautiful way to work toward and enjoy success!

My journey from then to now wasn't quick or easy. But it has allowed me to gain the knowledge necessary to develop the Inner Voice program and pave the way for others to identify their purpose; live it with passion; and be free of anger, anxiety, frustration, fear, doubt, guilt, and shame.

Inner Voice Whispers

What if the things you thought would hold you back actually provided you with new ways to move forward? What if, within your greatest annoyances, you could find your greatest effectiveness?

The problems that we must deal with today are essentially the same ones that humankind has dealt with since the beginning of time: problems with relationships, finances, work, rebellious children, and so on. Modern technology has certainly changed the way we live, but it hasn't changed human nature or the nature of our problems. The Inner Voice program is a new way to deal with these age-old problems efficiently and effectively, and it will work for you.

Here's something amazing that I've learned: Inner Voice principles and strategies could be considered totally selfish, because they're things you do for yourself, not for others. Think about this carefully. When we're nice to someone, it's not to help the person. When we're patient, kind, and caring, it's not for the other person. We do these things for ourselves, to develop our own characters, to keep moving along our own spiritual-growth paths—and, yes, to save our own lives. To think that we're doing things for others because they need it is to practice the character defect of arrogance. When we do the right thing, the biggest benefits go to us. Others might benefit to some degree, but we have far more to gain from our character assets—from being nice, caring, compassionate, generous, patient, and kind—than anyone else does.

But even though the Inner Voice program could be considered selfish because you benefit more than anyone else, it's not something you do alone—it's not an "I" program; it's a "we" program. Develop a circle of people who practice the Inner Voice way of life, and talk to them regularly. What I've learned from doing this is that it's very easy for me to see other people's problems, sometimes even more clearly than they do, and to share my experiences with them in a way that might help them. (Remember, I don't tell them what to do; I share my experience, strength, and hope.) And they do the same for me. I've given you example after example of that. When we get into the human defects of anger, anxiety, frustration, fear, and doubt, we're blinded by and to our own problems. When you feel this way, immediately make a call to someone who is Inner Voice experienced, and talk it out. Let that person help you restore your clear vision.

Remember how, when I explained how to do your own Discovery Chart, I shared what one of my mentors told me: "If you want what I got, you gotta do what I do"? Well, here's what I do—and how you can do it, too. It's the program I live every day.

1. Begin each day with gratitude. Thank your creator for all the good in your life. We'll always have challenges, but we'll also always have things for which we can be grateful. Sometimes it's a million-dollar deal, and sometimes it's simply a beautiful day. Be thankful.

2. Practice two-way conscious contact before the chaos of the day starts. Get out your journal and begin your two-way conscious contact by writing down your prayer or request or whatever you want to call it. It can be this simple: "Creator, direct me in my thinking today. Show me Your will for me and give me the wisdom, power, and courage to carry it out." If you're working on something in particular, it can be more specific. Then sit back,

Sharing the Message

I vividly remember the day I hit bottom. I'd been hiding behind an apartment complex, plotting my escape. I called a cab and, when it pulled up, made a dash to what I thought would be freedom. Before I could jump into the waiting car, I heard, "Stop! Police!" I was surrounded by officers with guns drawn. Slowly, I raised my hands and lowered myself to the ground so that they could arrest me.

At that moment, in more ways than one, I surrendered. I was empty, lonely, and in despair. I didn't want to live—but I wasn't dead.

I'd been in a downward spiral for years. I was a successful, admired athlete who'd managed to destroy every relationship and opportunity. I was like a wild juggernaut ripping through people's lives. I was selfish, I hurt my family and loved ones, and I ruined the trust of those closest to me.

Somewhere, deep inside me, was the awareness that there was a better way. Although I tried several times to get help and clean up my act, I couldn't make it stick— until, that is, I discovered the Inner Voice program. This is what I'd been yearning for my whole life, what I needed so that I could live the life I was meant for.

Today, I'm a new man. I know my purpose: to serve others who are experiencing the desperation I once knew, to show them how to acquire the gifts of hope and faith, to help them know the peace that is my life now.

— Henry,
life coach

relax, and wait for the answers to come. Write down the thoughts you get and test them: are they honest, pure, unselfish, and loving? If they are, you've got your plan for the day.

3. Recognize your responsibility. Thanks to the Inner Voice way of life, you may experience amazing abundance; but with abundance—whether it's material or spiritual—comes responsibility. Remember that "to whom much is given, much is expected."

4. Help others. Actively seek out ways to help others. Give financially, give emotionally, and give time.

5. Make progress. Become a little bit better every day. Living the Inner Voice way of life means that we don't place on ourselves the false burden of expecting perfection; we only expect progress.

6. Review, evaluate, and measure. Ask yourself every day, throughout the day, how you're doing. Take a daily inventory and do a weekly analysis, and plan so that you can keep making progress.

Inner Voice Whispers

You're not here to be the same as anyone else. Deep down, you have a dream. You have an inner voice nagging you about it. Don't ignore it. You are here for a purpose, and you won't get rest until you work toward it. Others are being cheated out of your greatness when you procrastinate.

7. Appreciate the power of being powerless. You can't control other people. You're powerless over most situations. Your part is to suit up; show up; bring your common sense, intelligence, and blessing to the day, every day; and leave the results to God. After you've done your part, relax and let God do His job.

8. Surrender. Do the best you can and then surrender it to a higher power. Turn it over, let it go, and listen for the answers. Let the inner voice work.

9. Reach out to other Inner Voice members. There's strength in numbers. When you're stuck, when you aren't sure what to do, when the message isn't coming through, when the alarm bells are sounding, connect with someone else who is living the Inner Voice way of life and knows how to help you work through your issues.

10. Share the Inner Voice gift. When people notice and comment on the change in your life, share the Inner Voice with them. Don't force it, don't try to sell them, but share what you've learned and what it's done for you.

So that's it. I started on this path more than five years ago, and it's been the greatest part of my life so far. If you're ready to give it a try, an entire community of Inner Voice members and I are here to help. We're changing the world one person at a time. Join us!

AFTERWORD

Well, here we are. It's the end of this book, but the beginning of an amazing journey for you. May I offer a few final words to get you on your way?

The Inner Voice movement is a pathway to a healthier, happier, more rewarding life. Inner Voice principles and strategies aren't something that we learn, do once, and finish. They're principles and strategies that we must continually apply, that we integrate into our daily routines, that become as habitual as breathing and eating. When you do this, you'll experience amazing results. You'll learn your reason for being here and develop a passion for the things that will help you live out your purpose. You'll intuitively know how to handle situations that used to baffle you. Instead of constantly fighting battles, you'll see gifts come your way without anxiety, frustration, fear, or doubt.

As I've developed and shared the Inner Voice way of life, I've noticed two clear patterns. Some people learn the program, understand the need for daily practice, put together a plan, connect with others, and find their lives improving every day. Others turn to their inner voice (usually after they've called me and I've walked them through it) and see great results, but, for whatever reason, don't implement the daily practice—and I don't hear from them again until they're dealing with the next crisis. That's usually two to three months later. That saddens me, because it doesn't need to be that way.

Think about it like this: If you're overweight and out of shape, and you want to lose weight and get fit, you're not going to see any notable results with just one meal of grilled fish and vegetables followed by a walk around the block. But if you adjust your lifestyle so that it includes regular low-fat meals with plenty of fruits and vegetables and daily exercise, over time you'll see the pounds come off and your overall health improve. The great news about the Inner Voice is that you'll see results from the daily practice of the program far quicker than you'll ever see from a diet and exercise program. For most people, the impact is immediate.

A Book That Had to Be Written

With my previous books on wealth building, I had a publishing contract signed and an advance check cashed before I wrote the first word. I'd written several drafts of *Inner Voice* without knowing how it was going to be published and distributed; I just knew I had to do it. I practiced the principles of powerlessness and surrender, and used two-way conscious contact to find out what I was supposed to do to share this life-changing message. I told God I was willing to produce the book at my own expense and give it away if that's what He wanted me to do. And within a few days, I had a commitment from Hay House to publish the book and give it worldwide distribution. It took a little longer to finalize the contract—that's just part of the process—but the publisher and I are both pleased with our agreement. About the same time, I finalized the agreement with a team to develop the e-learning program and the Personal Success Profile tool.

That's how the Inner Voice way of life works. We don't have to chase the answers; they come to us. We don't have to battle for the resources; they're readily available when the time is right. The proof is in your hands.

— Russ Whitney

This is why I'm extending a personal invitation to you to become part of the Inner Voice community: a community of like-minded people who are committed to finding and living out their purpose and, in the process, making life better for themselves and others.

You may also be interested in the e-learning platform my team and I have developed. It begins with a Personal Success Profile so that you can understand where you are in your journey from warrior to statesperson; then it provides the appropriate training modules that will help you advance and find your true purpose. To learn more about this extraordinary opportunity for spiritual development and about joining the Inner Voice community, visit www.InnerVoice.com/book.

When you live the Inner Voice way of life, there are absolutely no limits to what you can accomplish. I'm living proof of that—and so are the people who embraced the Inner Voice program with me as I was developing it and who joined the community later. Now it's your turn; this is your time. Seize it!

Thank you!
Are you ready to get started on your own Inner Voice
journey? Russ Whitney shares what to do next in this video:

www.innervoice.com/thanks

To get your free copy of Russ Whitney's e-book
Purpose to Passion in 21 Days,
visit www.innervoice.com/book.

INNER VOICE
CHARTS

Discovery Chart

INNER VOICE

Source of Anger	Who was involved? What happened?	The area(s) of my life this affects is/are:								I respond with these feelings and/or actions:						What I would like to say to or about who was involved or the situation:
		Pride, Feelings and Behavior	Dreams and Goals	Confidence and Self-respect	Security	Financial and Material	Relationships	Intimate Relationships	Overall Life Satisfaction	Fear	Dishonest and/or Deceit	Thoughtless and Uncaring	Self-centered	Impatient	Manipulative	

www.innervoice.com

Discovery Chart

INNER VOICE

What I would like to say to or about who was involved or the situation:

I respond with these feelings and/or actions:
- Manipulative
- Impatient
- Self-centered
- Thoughtless and Uncaring
- Dishonest and/or Deceit
- Fear

Overall Life Satisfaction

The area(s) of my life this affects is/are:
- Intimate Relationships
- Relationships
- Financial and Material
- Security
- Confidence and Self-respect
- Dreams and Goals
- Pride, Feelings and Behavior

Who was involved? What happened?

Source of Fear

Discovery Chart

INNER VOICE

Source of Resentment	Who was involved? What happened?	Pride, Feelings and Behavior	Dreams and Goals	Confidence and Self-respect	Security	Financial and Material	Relationships	Intimate Relationships	Overall Life Satisfaction	Fear	Dishonest and/or Deceit	Thoughtless and Uncaring	Self-centered	Impatient	Manipulative	What I would like to say to or about who was involved or the situation:

The area(s) of my life this affects is/are:

I respond with these feelings and/or actions:

www.innervoice.com

Weekly Character Asset Checklist

Starting Date: _____ / _____ / _____

(Start your week on the day that works best for you)

Each day, rate your behavior in each category using this scale:

> O = Doing well or making progress
>
> X = Need improvement in this area

At the end of the week, compare your ratio of "O's" to "X's" and use the Weekly Character Asset Analysis to evaluate your personal development.

CHARACTER ASSET/BEHAVIOR	S	M	T	W	T	F	S
Conscious contact with Inner Voice							
Honest with self							
Honest with others							
Open-minded							
Non-judgmental							
Complimentary, give credit, praise to others							
Discreet, respect confidences							
Polite, courteous, considerate							
Humble							
Grateful, not envious or jealous							
Moderate, not gluttonous							
Initiative, not lazy, not procrastinating							
Unselfish, generous							
Trusting							
Forgiving							
Sincere, straightforward, not manipulative							
Act with integrity and responsibility							
Kind, nice, not sarcastic							
Positive, optimistic							

www.innervoice.com

Weekly Character Asset Analysis

Top three areas in which I have made progress:

1. _____

2. _____

3. _____

Top three areas in which I need improvement:

1. _____

2. _____

3. _____

Action plan and notes to self for next week:

_____

_____

_____

_____

_____

_____

_____

Acknowledgments

My journey of the last five years has been anything but a solitary one. It's been full of old friends, new friends, renewed friends, teachers, advisors, coaches, and more—too many to name here. But at the risk of leaving someone out, I'm going to try to list the key people who were with me from the start and who helped me shape the Inner Voice program into what it is today.

Those amazing, generous people include the following:

José Oquendo; Herman Medeiros; Hugh Carlin, Jr., MSW, LSW; Cecilia Alailima, M.D.; Nicole Fisher; Bob Boye; Jeff Guminiak; Tony Capobianco; Kent Densley; Lee Lanktree; Tony Bellenger; Richie McCanna; Darrin Ginsberg; Pastor Dane Blankenship; Rabbi Yitzchok Minkowicz; Zalman Velvel; Kevin Harrington; Charlene Davis; Dennis Sullivan; Klaus-Uwe Kattkus, Ph.D.; Hellen Davis; Derrick Brown; and Mitch Huhem.

I also want to express my appreciation to Larry Benet, of SANG, for helping connect me with Reid Tracy of Hay House; to Reid Tracy for his commitment to this book, even when it was still in very rough-draft form; to Wendy Keller of Keller Media for her wonderful assistance with the nuts and bolts of the business side of the book; and to the editing and production team at Hay House.

Special thanks to the following:

Bill Bain, who tops the list of the special people without whom this book wouldn't be complete. Bill was the first person I hired at my first business 35 years ago. He's been a close friend and confidant, and has traveled with me through some fiery storms. His dedication to the Inner Voice way of life has been a godsend for me and for *Inner Voice*.

Cindy Barajas, whose dedication and willingness to share the depth of her spiritual knowledge helped move *Inner Voice* forward.

Will Trefethen, a multitalented man with a heart of gold, whose time and energy helped bring the *Inner Voice* message forward.

Jacquelyn Lynn, who worked with me on three of my previous books (four if you count the *Building Wealth* revision). Although the content is indeed mine, none of my books would have been books without her. When I started metamorphosing what I was learning into *Inner Voice,* I called Jackie; she intuitively knew that it wasn't ready and turned the project down. My inner voice told me to call her again last year. Impatiently humoring me, she agreed to look at my rough manuscript. A few days later, she called and said, "Russ, I want to be a part of this." In addition to her top-notch writing and organization skills, I appreciate that she reminds me to call on my own inner voice when I need an answer.

There are so many others—family members, friends, acquaintances, even strangers—who directly or indirectly contributed to what has become the Inner Voice way of life and message. I thank them all from the bottom of my heart and wish them the best that life has to offer.

— Namaste and Carpe Diem!
Russ

ABOUT THE AUTHOR

Entrepreneur, philanthropist and bestselling author **Russ Whitney** is a recognized worldwide leader in the business, real estate investment and financial training fields. A high-school dropout, Whitney began investing in real estate at the age of 21 while working full-time in a slaughterhouse. By the age of 23, he had achieved financial independence and was able to quit his job to concentrate on real estate. He became one of America's youngest self-made millionaires at the age of 27. His many business achievements include founding and building one of the largest and fastest-growing publicly traded financial-education companies of its type in the world.

Whitney is well known for his work with at-risk youths, having spearheaded a successful $2 million fundraiser to build the first youth centre in his hometown. Personally and through his companies, he has supported a wide range of charitable organizations, including domestic-violence shelters, youth programmes, Salvation Army services and more. As the developer of Monterey, Costa Rica, he spearheaded efforts to stock the local Red Cross medical centre with critical supplies, donating and transporting essential provisions.

After retiring from the day-to-day operations of his business ventures in 2008, Whitney launched a personal quest to find the answer to an age-old question: What is the true meaning of life? That five-year journey led to the creation of *Inner Voice*™, a unique programme for personal and spiritual development that's attracting followers from around the world.

In *Inner Voice: Unlock Your Purpose and Passion,* Whitney shares his humbling experiences and provides a step-by-step guide for learning and applying Inner Voice principles and strategies.

Whitney is the author of more than 30 books, workbooks and home-study courses, including the bestsellers *Building Wealth* (Simon and Schuster), *Millionaire Real Estate Mentor* (Dearborn) and *The Millionaire Real Estate Mindset* (Doubleday).

www.innervoice.com

Notes

Notes

Notes

Notes

Notes

Notes

Hay House Titles of Related Interest

YOU CAN HEAL YOUR LIFE, the movie, starring Louise L. Hay & Friends
(available as a 1-DVD programme and an expanded 2-DVD set)
Watch the trailer at: **www.LouiseHayMovie.com**

THE SHIFT, the movie,
starring Dr Wayne W. Dyer
(available as a 1-DVD programme and an expanded 2-DVD set)
Watch the trailer at: **www.DyerMovie.com**

O

BEING OF POWER:
The 9 Practices to Ignite an Empowerd Life,
by Baron Baptiste

THE COMPASSIONATE SAMURAI:
Being Extraordinary in an Ordinary World,
by Brian Klemmer

JUST GET ON WITH IT!:
A Caring, Compassionate Kick Up the Ass!, by Ali Campbell

STOP THE EXCUSES!:
How To Change Lifelong Thoughts,
by Dr Wayne W. Dyer

THE RICHES WITHIN:
Your Seven Secret Treasures,
by Dr John F. Demartini

All of the above are available at your local bookstore,
or may be ordered by contacting Hay House (see next page).

O

We hope you enjoyed this Hay House book. If you'd like to receive our online catalogue featuring additional information on Hay House books and products, or if you'd like to find out more about the Hay Foundation, please contact:

Hay House UK, Ltd.,
Astley House, 33 Notting Hill Gate,
London W11 3JQ • *Phone:* 0-20-3675-2450
Fax: 0-20-3675-2451
www.hayhouse.co.uk • **www.hayfoundation.org**

○

Published and distributed in the United States by:
Hay House, Inc., P.O. Box 5100, Carlsbad, CA 92018-5100
Phone: (760) 431-7695 or (800) 654-5126
Fax: (760) 431-6948 or (800) 650-5115
www.hayhouse.com®

Published and distributed in Australia by: Hay House Australia Pty. Ltd.,
18/36 Ralph St., Alexandria NSW 2015 • *Phone:* 612-9669-4299 • *Fax:* 612-9669-4144
www.hayhouse.com.au

Published and distributed in the Republic of South Africa by: Hay House SA
(Pty), Ltd., P.O. Box 990, Witkoppen 2068 • *Phone/Fax:* 27-11-467-8904 • www.
hayhouse.co.za

Published in India by: Hay House Publishers India, Muskaan Complex, Plot No.
3, B-2, Vasant Kunj, New Delhi 110 070 • *Phone:* 91-11-4176-1620 • *Fax:* 91-11-4176-1630
www.hayhouse.co.in

Distributed in Canada by: Raincoast, 9050 Shaughnessy St., Vancouver, B.C.
V6P 6E5
Phone: (604) 323-7100 • *Fax:* (604) 323-2600 • www.raincoast.com

○

Take Your Soul on a Vacation

Visit **www.HealYourLife.com®** to regroup, recharge,
and reconnect with your own magnificence.
Featuring blogs, mind-body-spirit news, and life-changing
wisdom from Louise Hay and friends.

Visit **www.HealYourLife.com** today!

Free e-newsletters
from Hay House, the Ultimate
Resource for Inspiration

Be the first to know about Hay House's dollar deals, free downloads, special offers, affirmation cards, giveaways, contests, and more!

 Get exclusive excerpts from our latest releases and videos from *Hay House Present Moments*.

 Enjoy uplifting personal stories, how-to articles, and healing advice, along with videos and empowering quotes, within *Heal Your Life*.

 Have an inspirational story to tell and a passion for writing? Sharpen your writing skills with insider tips from *Your Writing Life*.

Sign Up Now!

Get inspired, educate yourself, get a complimentary gift, and share the wisdom!

http://www.hayhouse.com/newsletters.php

Visit www.hayhouse.com to sign up today!

 HealYourLife.com

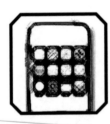